Surf Your Biowaves

Surf Your Biowaves

Use your biorhythms to bring you success

PETER WEST

quantum

LONDON • NEW YORK • TORONTO • SYDNEY

quantum

An imprint of W. Foulsham & Co. Ltd.

The Publishing House, Bennetts Close,
Cippenham, Slough, Berkshire, SL1 5AP, England.

ISBN 0-572-02497-5

This edition is an updated, revised and enlarged
version of a book originally published as
Biorhythms: Your Daily Guide to Achieving Peak Potential.

Printed in Great Britain by St Edmundsbury Press Ltd, Bury St Edmunds, Suffolk

Contents

Introduction

From the day you are born, a continuous range of cycles and rhythms recurs in a never-ending interchange of serial succession within the tiniest cells of your body, in your organic make-up, behavioural attitudes and environment.

The human body is so attuned to this succession of patterns – the lungs and breathing, the kidneys and their functions, the heart and its beating, day and night, spring, summer, autumn and winter – that, more often than not, we accept them without thinking. Some we fight, and there must be more we do not even know about yet, but rarely do we recognise any of them as cyclic events.

Among our bodily rhythms are three clearly defined cycles that affect our behavioural patterns but that have no cause and effect as such; they are simply continuous physiological changes. It is with these three cycles that this book is primarily concerned.

The Three Biorhythmic Cycles

Collectively, these cycles are popularly called biorhythms. Individually, they are known as the physical cycle, which has a duration of 23 days; the emotional or sensitivity cycle, with a periodicity of 28 days; and the intellectual cycle of 33 days.

These three cycles control performance in three distinct areas of behaviour. However, it must be stressed that they have no direct cause and effect in themselves but, in each case, are subject to the conditions of the environment prevailing at the time.

It has been found that there is a correlation between the state of the individual rhythm and certain factors in our behaviour. More to the point, awareness of the stage or phase of the rhythm gives the individual an opportunity to correct or adjust their conduct accordingly. The success rate following such action has been phenomenal.

Thus, these biorhythmic cycles offer a potential answer to our 'on' and 'off' days. The intelligent use and awareness of the phase of the rhythms can provide a more positive approach to life and, after a very short time, you will begin to feel far better in yourself.

Biorhythms do not indicate that at a specific time you will have an accident, throw in your job or win the Lottery. They do, however, indicate your potential physical ability, emotional sensitivity or mental acuity on any particular day.

What you do with this information is, of course, the key to the whole concept of biorhythms. What use, if any, you make of the information that biorhythms provide about your capabilities or limitations in each of the three cycles at any given time is entirely a matter of personal choice.

Each cycle begins its individual rhythm on the day you are born and remains constant until the day you die. Because of this regularity, the phase or stage of each rhythm can be calculated quite easily for any particular day, past, present or future. All that is needed is your date of birth.

For some people this is a point where a comparison with astrology inevitably arises although, as yet, there is no discovered relationship, if any exists, between the disciplines. However, both subjects are concerned with the individual and both can suggest which paths or attitudes to adopt.

Astrology advises in more specific terms, though it is often couched in nebulous phrasing. Biorhythms only provide information about capabilities and limitations, although the method of doing so is quicker than in astrology. For some individuals, biorhythms appear to be more accurate, but this should not be taken as a comment or slight against astrology or astrologers; the concepts are vastly different.

There is no hidden, occult magic involved in biorhythms. Their use is, quite simply, an exercise in calculating a physiological function and relating the results to our behavioural patterns in the light of research.

Once the results of biorhythmic theories emerged, it was only a question of time before the whole concept became subjected to many other experiments. Not the least of these, and certainly one of the most popular, has been in the field of compatibility studies.

Compatibility

In order to exist, we must get along with others to the best of our abilities. This is not always easy, however. We sometimes find ourselves behaving irrationally towards someone we meet for the first time; something does not quite 'click' into place. When this happens, our relationship does not get off to a very good start. In other cases, we immediately get along as though we had always been friends; there is a noticeable rapport.

Even those we have known for a long time occasionally appear to rub us up the wrong way. At first glance it may seem that our personal biorhythms are not compatible for socialising although, when we check them, we are surprised to find that it is the best possible day for a get-together. On other occasions, although our biorhythms indicate that we should not be talking to a particular person, somehow we are lifted out of our depression by the sheer magic of their personality. Or are we?

By comparing the biograms of individuals, it is possible to see how we ought to get along with others. It is not infallible by any means, but something like 90 per cent of the time we can see why we cannot get along with one person, but we can get along with another. Biorhythms do not have all the answers, but they can, and often do, provide an illuminating insight into the whys and wherefores of a relationship.

Your personal biogram reveals your potential behaviour patterns. It therefore follows that what it does for you, it must do for others, so the logical step is to compare them. This exercise provides virtually limitless possibilities in terms of human behavioural patterns and potential compatibility which are both exhaustive and exciting.

Another field in which the intelligent use of biorhythms has been gainfully employed is safety, particularly on the factory floor and in all forms of transportation. The success rate in this area has proved almost unbelievably high, with masses of statistical evidence to prove the validity of utilising biorhythms to reduce accident figures.

The sporting arena has been another success story. Trainers and managers alike have become tremendously enthusiastic following improved results from the athletes in their charge once biorhythms have been studied and the conclusions acted upon.

With a little imagination, there are very few areas where the application of biorhythms cannot be successfully employed.

In this introduction I have tried to whet your appetite for what is to come. By the time you have read this book, you will have all the information necessary should you want to take the subject further and experiment with biorhythms for yourself. I think you will.

Peter West

1

The Theory and Development of Biorhythms

From the dawn of time, all manner of life has responded to the natural cycles that influence us all, whether from within our bodies or from external sources. The most basic cycle, night and day, has been obeyed by most animals, human beings included, by sleeping in sheltered spots either at night if a diurnal creature, or by day if nocturnal.

Gradually we have become aware of other rhythms and cycles, the most natural of which, the seasons, follows on from day and night. In spring, new life appears in the animal and plant kingdoms; in summer, life flourishes and grows in abundance; in autumn, some life forms begin their specific annual preparation for death or hibernation in response to the cold of coming winter.

Not all forms respond to this basic periodicity, however. There are some creatures that flourish during the winter months, taking on the appearance of a totally different animal during this period.

An example is the stoat (called ermine in northern regions). One and the same creature in reality, it manifests differing responses to its natural rhythms according to the season. As the seasons change, so does this animal's outward appearance. This change does not occur haphazardly. A definite, traceable pattern exists, for there are distinctive changes in the ermine's life cycle that may be traced accurately by observation which, in turn, can be checked against statistical evidence recorded over a long period of time.

If this cyclic information is transcribed into graph form and constantly updated, the changes which occur are much more easily discernible. Eventually, the complete ermine/stoat life cycle will emerge in such a predictable manner that the overall picture can be observed and absorbed by anyone.

Behavioural Patterns in Man

The development of cyclic behaviour in human beings should not, however, be confused with our natural rhythms. Behavioural patterns are those that evolve from the way in which we live. When recorded, these have produced some startling statistics, illustrated by the following crime information collated in the period between the First and Second World Wars.

Compiled from the police files of over 2,000 American cities and towns over a period of five years, this information indicated a curious link between seasonal changes and crime patterns. So much so, that J. Edgar Hoover, one-time director of the FBI, was reported as saying that meteorologists could predict rapes as well as storms, though to a limited degree, of course.

Crime patterns varied very little from year to year. More murders were committed during the months of July and August than at any other time, particularly during the weekends. Over 60 per cent of these murders took place between 6 p.m. and 6 a.m. Burglary, however, was a different proposition. Between 6 p.m. and 2 a.m. on a Saturday in December, January or February was the favourite time.

The month of May saw very little crime, except for an upsurge in dog bites, more being recorded during this month than in any other. June was the peak month for suicides and admissions to hospitals – and for marriages. More cars were reported stolen in February and November than in any other month. The list of similar examples is endless.

Some 3,000 years ago the Greek physician, Hippocrates, noted that we appeared subject to good days and bad. We do not know if any serious study was made as to the reason for this, but we do know this assumption was recorded as being irrespective of whether one was ill or not. It is quite probable that this theory had been expounded earlier but was not noted because it was regarded as less important then than now to know about these good and bad days.

Hermann Swoboda

Shortly before the end of the nineteenth century, Hermann Swoboda, a professor at the University of Vienna, became aware of a slight regularity in certain human attitudes. He watched, waited and observed. At last, among other equally important discoveries, he realised that there was a definite rhythmic periodicity which seemed to affect human beings and their behavioural patterns.

Professor Swoboda continued his research in order to establish whether this phenomenon could be predetermined in some way by calculation. He then set out to prove the existence of a 23-day cycle which affected human physical and behavioural reactions. Research has refined his findings about this cycle.

At about the same time, Swoboda also discovered a 28-day cycle of emotional reaction and behaviour. This second rhythm was not as easily discernible as the first, because it sometimes coincided with the menstrual cycle in women. However, as the same periodicity was observable in men, Swoboda set to work to establish that such a definite pattern existed, irrespective of women's natural rhythm. His painstaking research was rewarded by convincing evidence that these rhythms of life did exist.

Although he was primarily a psychologist, Hermann Swoboda was naturally analytical and systematic and, once he was convinced of his findings, he published his first book, *Periodicity in Man's Life*, followed by *Studies in the Basis of Psychology*. He also devised a very basic measuring system and an instruction booklet, *The Critical Days of Man*, to supplement it. The study of biorhythms had been born.

Wilhelm Fliess

In a sense, biorhythms had two parents – and neither was aware of the other at the birth. By a strange coincidence, during roughly the same period as Swoboda was conducting his research from a psychological point of view, another doctor was amassing similar information from the standpoint of a practising physician.

Wilhelm Fliess, a Berlin nose and throat specialist, had observed the 23- and 28-day cyclic behavioural patterns for himself. He was the first to identify, or at least to announce publicly, the connections between biorhythms and behavioural patterns.

His beliefs were founded upon the simple theory that each of us inherits both male and female characteristics and that everyone therefore possesses a trace of bisexuality. Fliess firmly believed that there was a connection between his findings, evolution and life itself, yet his book, *The Course of Life*, went largely unrecognised at the time.

It was dismissed as too complex and mathematical to understand, but this did not prevent Fliess from continuing his researches. He realised the importance of his discoveries and discussed them frequently with another giant of the time, Sigmund Freud. Indeed, Freud was so convinced of the validity of Fliess's work that he used his colleague's theories in his own practice. During the development of Freud's now famous psychoanalytical ideologies, the Fliess theories were frequently referred to and employed.

Early Scepticism

However, these were the early days of biorhythmic research. As with most new ideas and theories, the struggle for acceptance was hard. Even today, we sometimes find it difficult to cope with the newest theories published in some fields of endeavour. It must have been far from easy during those early days of discovery to persuade others to accept the researchers' findings.

In the past hundred years or so, our scientific knowledge has advanced significantly. Take, for example, computer technology: only 40 to 50 years ago, a machine capable of the same functions as the pocket calculator which most of us now carry around would have occupied a space four or five metres square. With the silicon chip revolution now fully established, one may be forgiven for sometimes wondering where technology will lead.

In the early part of the twentieth century, new theories were almost always initially treated with a mixture of prejudice, scorn and suspicion, before even minimal acceptance was achieved. Fliess and Swoboda had much to contend with but, despite traces of grudging acceptance here and outright repudiation there, they continued to build on their respective theories. They both produced huge amounts of documentation and statistics.

Swoboda's massive work, *The Year of Seven*, contained mathematical analyses of the 23- and 28-day rhythmic repetitions displayed by subjects through several generations. It was vast in concept and represents the foundations on which modern biorhythmics are based.

Alfred Teltscher: Establishment of the Third Cycle

Wilhelm Fliess died in the late 1920s, about the time the third biorhythmic cycle was recognised. This time the theorist was not a doctor but an engineer and student of mathematics, Alfred Teltscher.

While no real hard evidence stems authoritatively from Teltscher himself, it seems that he established the pattern for the 33-day cycle after investigating the reasons for the variations in his students' intellectual capacity. He found there were predetermined periods when people demonstrated poor perception and performance in their intellectual pursuits and, equally, periods when they could more easily grasp new concepts, perform well and generally exhibit intellectual acuity.

Further to this, Dr Rexford Hersey and Dr Michael John Bennett of Pennsylvania University conducted similar research and, quite independently, arrived at similar conclusions about the 33-day cycle. So, once again, a curious coincidence occurred in the discovery and study of biorhythms.

Early Complexity of Calculations

However, as with the recognition of the two previous rhythms, nothing happened immediately. The utilisation of biorhythms remained neglected for a long time, only occasionally referred to in the ensuing years. One of the many reasons for this neglect may have been the seemingly complicated methods of calculation necessary for verifying the stages or phases of the cycles. None of the original pioneers seems to have been able to simplify the methodology in a way which would have proved acceptable to the layman and professional alike.

Yet, in practice, the calculations are very simple. We merely calculate the number of days that the subject has been alive. Counting the birth date as one, all that is needed is the total number of days from the date of birth up to and including the day in question. The total is divided by the number of days in the required cycle: that is, 23 days for the physical, 28 days for the sensitivity and 33 days for the intellectual. The remainder figure resulting from these divisions evaluates the stage of the individual rhythm; if there is no remainder, the day in question is the start of the new cycle.

Yet there appears to have been a stumbling block or mystery attached to this area of biorhythmic study. Admittedly, some clumsy attempts at a satisfactory formula were made: slide rules were produced by various individuals and sets of complicated tables were published by those interested in the theory of biorhythms, or intrigued by the mathematical challenge presented by the problem.

Whatever the reason, interest declined. With the exception of a few dedicated individuals, the whole thing seemed to lurk in the pending file until, in 1939, interest was again aroused as the result of a new publication.

Hans Schwing

In 1939, Hans Schwing, of the Swiss Federal Institute of Technology based in Zurich, produced a 78-page treatise in a comparative study of accidents and accidental death statistics. This work did not lead to a revival of interest in biorhythms as such, but it did spark some public interest. In the next 20 years or so came a spate of similar dissertations.

These all provided many interesting advances in the theories and, in some cases, proved that the time of birth might be valuable in assessing biorhythmic phasing but, once again, the inevitable comparisons with astrology arose.

This particular period saw a strong interest in astrology, again among a few dedicated adherents who were much more interested in the validity of a system than in the end product. Until very recently, astrology had not been regarded as a respected science or art (call it what you will), nor did the study of biorhythms attract the research it warranted.

Once again, it has to be stressed there is still no correlation between the two studies, except that we now accept the invaluable proof of periodic or cyclic behavioural patterns that affect us all, whether regarded from the astrological or biorhythmic standpoint.

New Interest in Biorhythms

A low-key public interest in biorhythmic studies was once again shown, occasionally interrupted by an odd publication or two. However, there seems to be little reason for the sudden explosion of popularity that the subject has enjoyed in the last 20 years or so. Now, there is hardly a country in the world that does not have at least one biorhythm society or association. In the last few years public interest in Great Britain, for example, has developed enormously, though it has not quite reached the same level of interest as in America, where, for a few cents, one can obtain a weekly forecast from a slot machine.

In Great Britain there are, however, several respected and well-conducted research programmes and publications, with some occasional publicity in newspapers, to help the cause. One magazine still offers a readers' biorhythm service for a very reasonable fee; it enjoys a remarkable response rate, with requests for 'repeat orders' a regular feature.

Thus, a hundred years or so on from the original discovery of the concept, we now have an established and respected study and practice which, provided it is properly employed, can and does lead to very significant improvements in the way we conduct our lives.

How, then, do these rhythms affect us, how are they determined and what exactly are they?

The Phases

It is of paramount importance to realise that the three cycles of biorhythms, irrespective of their phase, do not have a cause and effect in themselves. Fundamentally, they are continuous physiological changes, and awareness of them can help you to plan your daily life much more effectively. Because of the phasing of these cycles, you will either tend to perform well or give less-than-average attention to matters of the moment subject to prevailing conditions.

Each rhythm begins on the day you are born and continues its individual course throughout life, ceasing only at death. Everyone has them and is subject to their influence, but a tiny percentage of people do not 'conform' to the established patterns all the time.

The first half of each cycle is the 'plus' – the ascending, developing, progressive period. Confident and aggressive, full of vim and vigour, with mental perception at a peak, you will perform well until you reach the zenith of your powers halfway through this first phase. Your capabilities tend to remain at this high level, then gradually tail off until the rhythm moves into the second half of its cycle.

The second phase is the rejuvenation period, similar to a recuperative period after an operation. This half of the cycle sinks to a nadir, again at the midpoint, then begins steadily to progress towards the positive phase once more until the cycle has been completed. The pattern is repeated continuously throughout life.

Critical Days

The days on which the cycles begin or move from one phase to the other are known as 'critical' days. Publicity about these days or, perhaps more accurately, the label 'critical' which has been applied to them, seems to have served to popularise biorhythms more than any other aspect.

It has been statistically proved that accidents are more likely to occur on these critical days than at any other point in the cycles. The probability of an accident occurring on these days is very high, whether through lowered physical vitality, irrational emotional behaviour or inferior mental perception causing the subject to be more accident-prone.

Each rhythm has three critical days: at its beginning, the start of the cycle; at the halfway stage, when it changes from the positive to the negative phase; and at the end of the cycle, which, of course, is also the beginning of the next positive phase.

There are other significant points in each of the cycles, which are detailed in the chapters dealing with the individual rhythms. The designation 'critical' is somewhat of a misnomer, however, because nothing critical does occur, except for the actual changes in the cycles.

In most aspects of life, transition from one phase to another may be termed a turning point, a psychological moment, which may be favourable and providential or, perhaps, disturbing, unlucky, inauspicious or unsuitable, depending on individual circumstances. Understanding that these various meanings can be applied to the critical days in your biorhythms will enable you to use them to advantage.

A change of job may, for example, be favourable in the long run, but it is also disturbing. When children leave junior school to attend senior school, it is a turning point in their educational careers, but it may also prove difficult because of the environmental changes involved.

A new manager may be appointed to head your department, shop or factory, at a psychological moment favourable or unfavourable to you. A change in a regular facet of life may, therefore, have an effect that can be determined in some cases, but only guessed at in others.

Abrupt changes are a different matter altogether, however. Let us assume that you return home each day in exactly the same way whatever the circumstances, irrespective of weather conditions, season or whatever. One day your regular train is cancelled, something that has never occurred before, or a party of tourists is occupying the carriage you normally sit in. Your immediate reaction will naturally be defensive, but it will manifest itself in different ways according to your individual personality. Despite the way in which you react in such a situation, you will be temporarily off balance.

Perhaps you have arranged to meet someone at a specific time and place, with no doubts that the details of the meeting are correct. You arrive a few minutes early but, after 20 minutes or so, realise that the other person is not going to arrive. Your most probable reaction will be one of temporary emotional disturbance and perhaps intellectual annoyance at suddenly being faced with unexpected alternatives in order to rectify an unfamiliar situation.

Maybe you have planned and worked very hard to produce a sales programme which you believe cannot fail because of the great number of hours you have spent verifying all the details. However, your boss rejects your scheme out of hand, either by qualifying this decision or perhaps not even bothering to give you a reason at all. Your inner reaction will leave you temporarily off balance.

Such everyday situations, and your reactions to them, are what critical days are concerned with. You are temporarily off balance during these transitional periods, which can last for between 24 and 48 hours: a long time to be off balance, even to a minor degree.

Suppose that one of the examples quoted above occurred while your biorhythms were in one of their transitional periods: you were experiencing a critical day, a double critical day or worse, a triple critical day. In such an event, your normal mode of behaviour could be swept aside in a moment of emotional irrationality, intellectual blindness or physical rage; you would be disturbed!

The Grand Triple Critical Day

There is one point in everybody's life when all three biorhythms reach the same phase and stage as the day of birth, and then restart their respective cycles in exactly the same patterns.

This 'grand triple critical day' occurs 21,252 days or 58.2 years (58 years and 66 or 67 days if an extra leap year is involved) from the date of birth. In this period, 924 physical cycles, 759 sensitivity cycles and 644 intellectual cycles have occurred. The figure 21,252 is arrived at by multiplying the number of days in each cycle together: $23 \times 28 \times 33$.

Until this point, each rhythm has had a succession of critical days, sometimes coinciding with the other rhythms passing from positive to negative phase at the same time, resulting in double or triple critical days, but without all three cycles reaching the identical point as on the day of birth.

There are at least six critical days each month, sometimes eight, in everyone's biorhythms. Allowing for the basic six occurring in an average month of 30 days, this means you are in a critical phase of your biorhythms for 20 per cent of the time, every month.

Emotional and Physical Double Critical Days.

During the grand biorhythmic span of 58.2 years, there are many occasions when a double critical day occurs in the emotional and physical rhythms and it is this particular combination which is statistically proven to coincide with the most accident-prone period.

Single critical days signal problems of their own, of course, because you are likely to be temporarily off balance on them, but the emotional/physical double critical days should be treated with more caution. Awareness of the inherent problems of these days may help prevent distress or accidents.

Simply checking back to a date when something went wrong has more than a 60 per cent probability of showing you were in a critical phase on that day. More to the point, you may even recall saying at the time that had you been 'aware' of certain information, the incident may not have happened.

Accuracy of the Birth Date

In the physical rhythm, the critical days are 1 and 12; in the sensitivity cycle, days 1 and 15; and intellectually, days 1 and 17.

There is a strong possibility that the date you are investigating may fall on either side of these critical days, but there could be a simple explanation for this. Your time of birth may have been very early in the morning and, while many doubt the validity of the actual birth time being important in this respect, others regard it as vital. There is some evidence that, where the timing of a critical day seems to be out by 24 hours, the time of birth is the best factor to consider. Similarly, a very late time of birth could have an effect in the opposite direction.

Alternatively, of course, it may be possible that you have the wrong date for your birthday. It may seem strange to make such a suggestion in this modern world with all its advanced technology, but it can and does happen all too often for the analyst to ignore the possibility. At this point, it would be wise to remember that biorhythms are not the be-all and end-all of accuracy. Errors can occur but, statistically, the chances are strong that they will not.

Using Biorhythms for Planning Ahead

Now let us consider how biorhythms can be utilised for planning ahead. If you have important dates or events coming up and wish to know your capabilities, it is a simple matter to check the particular phasing of your rhythms for that time and plan accordingly.

Should the relevant cycle appear unfavourable, allow for the possibility of error in your behavioural patterns or, if you can change the proposed date to a more favourable time, do so; a simple adjustment is all that is needed. Once again, there may be the inevitable comparison with astrology, but you should disregard this for no correlation is yet proven.

Despite all the advances which have been made in psychological analyses of behavioural patterns, an element of 'chance' could possibly enter the equation. However, to give some idea of the valuable potential of biorhythms and their use, let us return to the thesis of Dr Hans Schwing, which was published in 1939.

This report, an extremely accurate and precise analysis, was based on 700 accident cases, with a further 300 cases of deaths recorded in the city of Zurich's archives. Schwing set out to prove the validity of biorhythmic theory and its relationship to a detectable pattern, or cycle of life. Using the complete biorhythmic span of 21,252 days (23 × 28 × 33) as a basis, Schwing's calculations showed that there must be 4,327 days on which one of the biorhythms will be at a critical point, with the remaining 16,925 days being comprised of mixed rhythms. In percentage terms this was expressed as a ratio of 79.6 to 20.4.

Schwing demonstrated that 322 accidents were recorded on single critical days, 74 on double critical and 5 on triple critical ones. The remaining 299 accidents occurred on mixed-rhythm or normal days. Thus, nearly 60 per cent of accidents (401) fell on critical days, representing 20 per cent of the time, whereas only 40 per cent (299) fell on the remaining 80 per cent normal, non-critical days. Food for thought, indeed.

Another report, published in 1954, resulted from the study of 497 accidents involving agricultural machinery. The author of this report, Rheinhold Bochow of Berlin's Humbold University, found that only 2.2 per cent of the accidents fell on normal, or mixed-rhythm days.

However, 26.6 per cent fell on single critical days, 46.5 per cent on double critical days and 24.75 per cent on triple critical days. The astonishingly high percentages shown in this particular series of results spurred on other researchers to further study.

Applications of Statistical Evidence

If the results of these accident statistics were to be used as the basis for future analyses by, say, a small transport company, surely the possibility of accidents could be reduced? Drivers could be taken off the road on their most accident-prone days and given alternative work, or they could be taught the fundamentals of biorhythmic theory in order to become more aware of the potential hazards of particular days in their cycles.

A company with good employer/employee relationships could even work out a rest-day rota system so that no real hardship would be involved either in earnings or in the loss, however temporary, of personal prestige. This is exactly the sort of scheme which has been implemented by some companies all over the world.

All kinds of business concerns, not only those directly related to transportation, have used biorhythmic studies of their staff; the success rates achieved speak for themselves. Accident figures are down, the insurance companies are more than happy, management are delighted and personnel involved feel the better for it. All this had led to increased productivity – an additional bonus.

Other Uses of Biorhythms

Biorhythms can also be used effectively to check compatibility with others. We all want to get along as well as possible with other people, but this is not always easy to achieve. However, if there is a way of improving relationships, the obvious step is to use whatever method of improvement is available.

Your personal biograms reveal your potential behavioural patterns. It therefore follows that if they do so for you, they also do so for others. The logical next step is to compare them. In the field of biorhythmic compatibility studies, an astonishing success rate has been recorded once the basic principles have been understood and simple rules observed.

The use of biorhythms does not stop here, however. They can be used for diet courses, giving up smoking, improving sexual harmony, sporting successes, academic studies, effective holiday planning, redecorating, gardening – the list is endless.

Remember, once you have your biorhythms charted, you can live a far more positive life in every sphere, provided you work at it.

2

The Physical Cycle

The physical cycle is a 23-day rhythm in positive mode for the first half and negative mode for the second, with critical days at the change-over between one cycle and the next and at the halfway point.

This rhythm is concerned with all the physical phenomena of performance and capability. The range of possibilities and potential is enormous and, when considered alongside the other two rhythms, it still has a high rating. This is because whatever activity you intend to undertake, the physical ability to carry it through must be favourable for positive results to be achieved.

Sometimes the effects of this cycle are hardly noticeable, while at others they are painfully apparent, occasionally surprisingly so in the course of our normal daily routine.

It does not matter which day we choose, so let us start from the moment you hear the morning alarm. Your arm snakes out and shuts off the hideous noise, or it gropes blindly and dully. You leap out of bed, or you stagger.

The Positive Phase

If you are in the positive phase of this cycle, you should begin to wake up feeling good; men may be particularly aware of this. Shaving tends to be reasonably easy, irrespective of the method employed: the skin feels good, smooth and elastic. The blade glides over the face with far less chance of a nick and the skin's response to an astringent aftershave sets the tone for the day.

There is more chance of feeling like a light meal, at least when this cycle is in the plus phase and, depending on normal habits, what you eat will be well prepared; no burnt offerings today. The usual walk to the station scarcely has an effect. You notice that you pass others who, on other days, have passed you. You will not object to standing on the crowded train or even sitting in a non-smoking carriage even if you are a heavy smoker yourself. The walk from the station to the office, factory or other workplace is taken – literally – in your stride.

If you work in an office, you may experience slight restlessness and will not want to remain seated at your desk for too long at a time; you will use any excuse to get up and walk around. You will feel almost 'frisky', perhaps with a tendency towards irritability without knowing why. In fact, the cause will simply be a lack of exercise, and the short excursions you feel like making represent your need to work off an excess of physical well-being.

A manual worker will achieve all his or her tasks confidently and sometimes ahead of schedule which, if on an assembly line, could make them feel a little bored, again perhaps leading to a touch of irritability.

You will relish the lunch break more for the opportunity it provides to get some physical exercise than for eating. You will approach the journey home with even more zeal than usual and, when you get home, the slightest excuse to walk the dog, mow the lawn, redecorate or put some time in on the car will be welcome. Better still, a couple of hours spent playing football, tennis or other sport is just what is needed when you are in this positive phase of the physical cycle, with its attendant feelings of physical well-being.

The Negative Phase

In the negative phase, this story is reversed, of course. Getting up will be a struggle, staying up a bigger one. For men, shaving can be a hazardous affair because the skin will feel rough and wet shaving may produce a cut which, even if it is only a slight nick, will feel quite painful.

You may not feel like breakfast, you cannot bring yourself to eat a thing and may only just be able to swallow one cup of tea or coffee. The journey to the station seems too long; it could even take an extra five minutes the way you feel. Standing will be painful, and if you are a smoker, you will have to stand even if a seat is available in a non-smoking carriage because you simply must have a cigarette to keep up your flagging spirits. You will prefer the escalator or lift to the stairs and, if possible, you will wait for a bus rather than walk the rest of the way.

When you reach your workplace, you will sink gratefully into the nearest chair for, by now, all you want to do is collapse. Workloads, no matter how light, will take their toll. At lunch-time, even if you have been glued to your chair all morning, you will just want to rest. A few sandwiches will suffice and you may even want to put your head down for a short nap.

Somehow, you will struggle through the rest of the day, but come the time to go home you may even feel like staying the night just so you won't have to expend all that energy again!

Once at home, all you will want to do is sit down in front of the television. The dog can walk itself, the grass can grow, the household chores and the decorating can wait, the car can have its service another time. At the end of the evening, getting to sleep may be a little more difficult than usual but, once achieved and although deep, you may not feel as though you have had adequate rest when you wake up the following day.

These two comparisons may seem rather dramatic but, if you care to spend a short time thinking about it, you will remember having days like these yourself, though perhaps not quite so exaggerated. However, we all experience good days and bad. A systematic check will show we experience these in a cyclic pattern and that they run more or less on the lines described.

Just occasionally, certain days may stand out in the mind: maybe a day when you fell for no reason, seemed to have pulled a muscle carrying the shopping or slipped down the stairs while vacuuming.

This may have occurred while you were having a critical day and, unconsciously, falsely misinterpreted your capability. You may have agreed to go kite-flying with the children and overdone the exercise altogether. This is exactly what biorhythms are all about: determining your capabilities for any given day.

Reading the Biogram

Figure 1 shows a biogram for one month of 30 days, illustrating the duration of the physical cycle which, in this example, starts on the first day of the month.

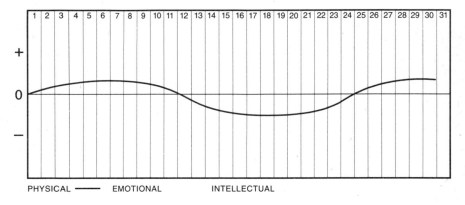

Figure 1. The physical cycle

Biograms such as this usually show all three rhythms together, with the lines drawn either in different colours or styles, so the exact stage of each rhythm can be compared against the others. This shows just one cycle so that we can discuss the physical cycle in particular. In our example, the physical cycle is in the seventh day of its new phase on the thirtieth day of the month.

The 'O' line indicates the norm although, as the cycle is continuous, there is no actual norm. The graph line either crosses the base line or is above or below it. In fact, the points at which the curve crosses the base line are the critical days.

So, straightaway we can see that there are going to be three critical days in this month, two when the cycle moves into the positive phase and one when it goes into the negative stage: on the 1st, 24th and 12th respectively.

Effects of the Positive Phase

The cycle in this example starts on the first day of the month and rises into the positive phase, achieving its maximum extent at day 7: the 'mini-critical' day. Physical abilities will be at maximum potential on this seventh-day peak and, if you are undertaking any form of special physical activity, you ought to be able to give your best performance then.

This is the stage of the positive phase where you should perform superbly well physically, although there is a risk that because you feel so good you may just possibly overdo things and cause physical injury or discomfort. There are many examples of the validity of the physical cycle's positive phase, but perhaps the most impressive is that of Mark Spitz, who won no less than seven gold medals for swimming in a very short space of time at the 1972 Olympics – six of which also set new world records.

Between 27 August, a rising critical day, through to the next critical day on 7 September, with the mini-critical day occurring on the 2 September, Mark Spitz achieved this unprecedented and still unequalled Olympic world record. (For the record, his emotional cycle was also in the plus phase, peaking to its mini-critical day on 1 September.)

Effects of the Negative Phase

In the negative phase, the lowest point of the cycle is reached on day 18. It is at this stage that the rhythm begins to turn once again into the positive phase, which it enters on day 24. Day 18 is also the most negative part of the cycle, the trough, when the mini-critical day occurs: the day of maximum lethargy with no energy and no inclination for anything active.

Athletics are not recommended on this day except for routine practice. It is often on this negative mini-critical day that people overreach their potential by trying to do far more than they are capable of: finishing the decorating or gardening, or trying to complete outstanding tasks that never seem to get done on schedule. These simple jobs are just the sort which are so often unsuccessfully attempted at this stage. For if there is going to be an incident or accident caused by or through any physical incapacity, this is the day of highest probability.

Making Necessary Allowances

Again, it must be stressed that biorhythms do not have a cause and effect in themselves, but are merely guidelines for timing events for the best results. There is no reason why you cannot perform all manner of physically strenuous tasks while in the negative stage or on critical or mini-critical days, provided that you allow for these particular conditions of the cycle.

After all, most sportsmen and sportswomen, especially professionals, have to compete continually; it is their livelihood. Most of them know their capabilities backwards, however, and are aware of cyclic behaviour patterns in their make-up. They know how to recognise and allow for temporary weakness during their off periods and also how to capitalise on their extra strengths when they are on form.

In football, for example, it is often reported that the centre forward is 'off form' because he misses the easy goals or other opportunities where he would ordinarily move in with his usual skills and win the moment. Or take the cricketer who consistently bowls erratically for a few days, or bats appallingly when he would normally have his hundred up; or the snooker player whose 'eye' is out when he would normally clear the table. All are examples of the kind of below-average performance which frequently occurs in the negative phase of the physical cycle.

It works in reverse as well. The champion may be off form and the outsider comes in from nowhere and beats them. Both are professionals, both are good, but the champion usually has the edge because of other skills. However, if the champion's rhythms are in the wrong phase when the opponent's are in the right one, the advantage will lie with the opponent. That is how new champions are made, and is one explanation of how someone may temporarily achieve fame by eclipsing the proven player at a fortuitous time, but subsequently proving unable to maintain the new position.

Applying the Biogram

By charting your personal biorhythms and noting their phasing you can, with relatively minor adjustments, achieve better results, which must inevitably lead to a better way of life. The theory and practice of biorhythms can be applied in all aspects of life.

In early spring, the garden begins to beckon; it needs to be turned over and generally tidied up. At the same time, the house would probably be transformed with spring cleaning. Looking at Figure 1 again, it is obvious that the best time for both jobs would be between the 2nd and the 11th or between the 25th and 30th. However, there is no reason why you cannot do this work on other dates, that is between the 13th and 23rd, provided you realise you will not have the same capabilities as in the first two periods. Allow for this, do not overdo it, and jobs like this become easier to take on and complete – safely!

Physiological Basis of the Physical Rhythm

In all probability the physical rhythm relates to basic muscle fibres and, as everything in our bodies has a rhythm or definite cyclic existence, it may be that everything to do with our physical capabilities culminates in the expression of the physical rhythm. We all have biological clocks and we all do respond to them.

Some people vary from the norm; they seem to be out of step with the rest of their immediate circle. This may be observed in the phenomenon of 'day' people and 'night' people, or 'morning' and 'evening' people. Their personal clocks are the same as everyone else's, but they appear brighter or physically more active at different times of the day. Every one of us responds to our personal 'inner' clock in exactly the same manner, but the timing may differ.

In many cases this can be traced to the time of birth. Often people born after noon are 'night' people, who seem to come alive around 10 or 11 p.m. and stay this way through the night to the early hours. It is rare for those born in the early hours to like the early hours in practice, but this is not an infallible rule.

There are some exceptions, but it could account for many personal foibles.

It is no good playing a round of golf if you start by feeling tired and finish exhausted and irritable. It would be far more sensible to suggest to your partner that nine holes would be better because you feel under par. They might be more amenable, knowing that you are at least prepared to make the effort, even if they do not know why.

This is half the battle of successful relationships and improving compatibility with those around you. Compromise, a dirty word to some, is always effective when used in such a judicious manner. Both parties want to enjoy themselves, so try to arrange the maximum pleasure possible in the right atmosphere at the right time. Simple adjustment is far better than an outright refusal.

The Health Factor

In the negative phase of the physical cycle, a strong health factor is involved. You are far more prone to catch chills or colds or get indigestion because of inadequate or irregular meals, upsetting your normal, regular, personal body functions as a result.

During this phase you are more susceptible to pain and more likely to bleed more freely in the event of injury; you recover more slowly than usual from illness. In fact, so much so, that some doctors time operations to coincide with the plus phase of your physical rhythm to facilitate recovery. Pain is then easier to cope with and your body is in better shape all round. Post-operative shock to the body is serious and in some cases can kill, but this is considerably lessened if such time factors are taken into account.

Some patients on supervised courses of drugs may need to be strictly informed of dosage and dosage times on these negative days. It has been found that the old idea of 'three times a day after meals' can be very dangerous in certain circumstances. Doctors now know that what in some cases might be acceptable to our bodies at, say, 8 a.m. can be positively lethal at 4 p.m.

Power Surges

We all recall those occasions when we have felt out of sorts at about four or five in the afternoon, dreading the idea of having to meet a long-standing social obligation later in the evening, and wondering how we are going to cope. Later that same evening, we suddenly realised that though we were half dead three or four hours earlier, we are now on top of the world: we simply do not feel the same person.

There are several possible reasons for this. Normal pulse variations during the 24-hour period may be responsible. If the average rate is 72 beats per minute, in the evening it may be higher or lower by as much as ten beats, making a considerable difference in our physical responses. The majority of us are at our lowest ebb in the early hours, even if we are 'night owls'; we bear little resemblance to the active person of 12 hours earlier or later when we are virtually at the opposing peak.

Another reason for a dramatic change in our responses could be the 12 hours or so when we experience the critical day change period. It has been reported by some people that they feel a surge of power, albeit brief, when their physical critical day moves from the negative to the positive stage; when switching from the positive to the negative, they experience a short period of extreme fatigue, lethargy or temporary indolence.

Others have marked a critical day in their diary, often without knowing anything about biorhythms, as the day when they suffered a bad bout of indigestion because of poor meals or poor timing of meals. They perhaps ate the wrong things, just making do with a stodgy sandwich when their body was crying out for a square meal. This is a major fault with many long-distance lorry drivers, who tend to get the job or distance done rather than take time out for a meal.

Even without a knowledge of biorhythms, it makes sense to have good meals at regular intervals so that the body can maintain a steady stamina flow. Failure to do so, especially when driving regularly, is often the first step towards creating the potential for an accident.

Taking Care in the Negative Phase

If normal stamina is low on a physical critical day and a meal is missed or just a snack grabbed, mental responses are likely to become dulled. In the event of quick reactions becoming necessary, only a half-hearted response is likely: in extreme moments, this may be the difference between life and death. Excessive smoking when not eating regularly also tends to dull normal reflexes.

As a substitute for a meal, heavy smoking often causes headaches and, when these occur during the negative phase, the body has no reserves to fall back on. It is a little like hitting someone when they are down, only in this case carelessness can actually kill.

Equally worthy of attention on such days are drinking habits – and not just alcohol. The body requires minimum and maximum amounts of liquid, varying according to individual needs. A lack of care in dietary matters will affect sleeping habits. When you fail to take care in the negative phase of the physical rhythm, you are in effect punishing your body even more.

None of us is perfect and it is not always possible to take the rest and eat the diet we should. Occasional lapses should not cause much harm, but they can create unnecessary problems for some. Whenever possible, if you can maintain a correct attitude, especially at critical times, you will help your body to function properly. Regular meals, moderate exercise and the establishment of routine habits to conform with your biorhyhmic patterns will increase your capabilities and achievements.

Those who suffer from rheumatism, arthritis or asthma may find it easier to avoid attacks by keeping a discerning eye on their physical cycle, especially if adverse or uncertain weather conditions are forecast. People with high blood pressure or heart conditions should avoid driving for too long when their biorhythms are in an adverse phase. In these conditions, you should never drive on an empty stomach because the resultant lowering of blood sugar can make you accident-prone.

Reading the Signs

Knowing that your potential is low alleviates some of the tension otherwise encountered and can lessen the probability of problems arising. However, if they should occur, just being able to read the danger signs and make the necessary adjustments in plenty of time becomes easier.

Driving, especially, may become hazardous on critical days, even if you are not the initial cause of an accident. Reactions are all the poorer on critical days irrespective of whether the cycle is passing from the negative to the positive or from the positive to the negative phase.

Those who sense that small surge of power on negative to positive change-over days often speak of a tremendous feeling of well-being and physical bonhomie. In fact, they may be lulled into a false sense of ability and their judgement may become faulty as a result. Similarly, long spells at the wheel on the reverse critical day can also take its toll, because you fail to notice just how much energy is draining from your body. On these days, wearing a seat belt proves its real worth and helps combat fatigue. On long-distance journeys it is surprising just how much the body moves when freely seated. Wearing a seat belt restricts the body movement considerably: energy is conserved that might otherwise be frittered away non-productively.

Educating the mind to the capabilities of the body is reasonably easy for most people. Despite our occasional lazy streak, nearly all of us will sometimes overdo things if unusual tasks need to be carried out. These are just the occasions when accidents are most likely to happen. We become so caught up with the matter in hand that the little things can pass us by. We tend not to notice or choose to ignore those little aches and pains, and simply put them down to unaccustomed physical activity. We are right, but we forget that these are part of the body's natural early-warning system.

Swimming is a good example. It takes far more out of us than we fully appreciate. On critical days, we should be very careful indeed; not just because cramp may set in and temporarily incapacitate us, but because the blind panic that ensues often causes the victim to drown in such circumstances.

The two are inextricably linked: if we had not overdone the one, we may not have experienced the other extreme. There are more cases of drowning on double critical days, that is the physical/emotional or physical/intellectual days, than at any other time. With a little thought, many might still be alive today.

Overstepping the Limit

Many of us live on nervous energy, dismissing the physical limits we think we may easily ignore but, sooner or later, there comes a time of reckoning. Careful monitoring of the physical cycle can alleviate a lot of the unnecessary stress which we could well do without. We live in stressful times, and stress is a killer. In simple terms, stress may be caused by merely failing to realise how we are driving ourselves (or being driven) beyond limits we often fail to recognise.

Coming to terms with this problem is not always easy. Our present way of living, especially in towns and cities, involves a lot of stress. The bus is cancelled or late and, when it does eventually arrive, you are unable to board because it is full. Your boss asks too much of you but you cannot or will not say no. Friends ask for help when you really do not feel like giving it, but you do. You ask someone to do you a favour and they refuse, resulting in a little more stress.

These are the sort of times when you really should monitor your physical welfare. When in the negative phase, try to ease off as much as you can and, when in the positive stage, try not to overdo things.

There are so many ways in which your physical rhythm alone can be used to best advantage. Remember, you do not have to stop enjoying things just because your rhythm is in its negative phase for about ten days or is at critical point; all you need do is ease off the pressure, to compensate the body for its lack or over-abundance of energy.

Once you enter into the swing of things and start to enjoy the new routine, it will soon become second nature to use your biorhythms intelligently. Prepare for the negative phases and take life at a steadier pace while they last. Make extra-special efforts on the critical and mini-critical days. During the positive periods, make the most of your capabilities – capitalise all the way, but sensibly.

There will be a few occasions when you may not be able to make the simple adjustments you would like, but at least you will know just how far you can safely go. That, in itself, must be reward enough.

3

The Emotional Cycle

The 28-day emotional cycle, also known as the sensitivity rhythm, is concerned mainly with mood, sensitivity and social ability. It is the easiest rhythm to chart, but probably the most difficult of the three to contend with and, for a variety of reasons, is also the most misunderstood.

Because of its duration, which coincides with lunar phasing in astrology, it is frequently a starting point in any comparisons between biorhythms and astrology. The correlation, though, is a vague one. Nor is there any relationship between this rhythm and the female menstruation cycle, even if the two may coincide for a while, because this particular cycle never varies, but the female rhythm does.

Emotional Critical Days

Like the physical cycle, the emotional rhythm starts off with a critical day, has its transition day from positive to negative 14 days later and ends on the third critical day 14 days after that. It, too, has mini-critical days. The first occurs on day 8 in the positive phase and at day 22 in the negative stage.

Because of this phasing, those born on a Monday will always have alternate Mondays marking the peaks and troughs in their cycle and the attendant behaviour patterns associated with them, while every other Monday will be a critical day. This could account for the 'favourite day' theory. Not everyone will find this idea appealing, but it is surprising how much of a guide it can prove when deciding which are good, or bad, days.

On an emotional critical day, you are at your most susceptible to a variation of emotional reactions, irrespective of the direction of the rhythm at the time. You may demonstrate irritability, insensitivity or even irrationality in the response you show to almost any situation. Differing environmental situations will not make much difference at such times although, in normal circumstances, environment and prevailing conditions are taken into account before determining response.

Even the calmest of people have been known to explode at the critical psychological moment; conversely, the most volatile have been known to pass through this period without raising an eyebrow.

As this rhythm controls everything to do with emotional response at all levels, it takes on an added importance in relationships, potential accident situations or anything requiring drive and enthusiasm. There really is little point in giving a party if it coincides with day 22 of the emotional cycle, a physical negative stage and intellectual critical day, as even the most cynical of critics would appreciate.

However, should an adverse situation like this arise, and nothing can be done to change it, such a social event could still take place as long as its limitations are recognised and the individual concerned makes a serious attempt at remaining on an even keel.

The Emotional Positive Phase

Governed largely by the nervous system, this cycle was described by Wilhelm Fliess as the manifestation of the cells influencing the feminine inheritance in our make-up. The first half of the emotional rhythm relates to the plus or positive phase, when we are more cheerful, responsive and optimistic.

This period is favourable for all creative enterprises, romance, friendship and co-operation generally. Co-ordination also plays an active part in this cycle; the nervous system has to 'feel' that things are right before this will be apparent. In fact, co-ordination is markedly absent during the negative phase.

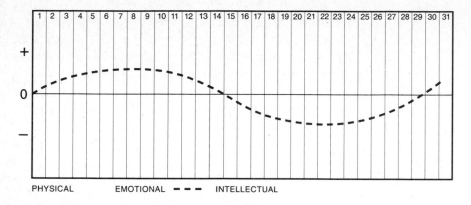

Figure 2. The emotional cycle

By the eighth day of the positive phase, the individual's sense of well-being and sociability peaks and, at this point in the emotional cycle, sensitivity is at its highest. However, on a mini-critical day, there is a risk of becoming overconfident and overdoing things because of the way you feel. After this stage, the rhythm curves down towards the critical day halfway through the cycle, and your performance, while still good, begins to lose its edge.

The Critical Day

On the critical day itself almost anything can happen if emotive issues generate any kind of stress. Of the three rhythms, the emotional is the one most likely to predispose you to error and accident. Your thinking is coloured by your emotional reactions to what is going on around you.

You may start the day well but if the slightest thing upsets you, it is possible for the Third World War to begin: you may become ultra-touchy and oversensitive without fully realising it. If you are driving and you are overtaken by another vehicle, you could chase after it just to overtake the other driver in turn. It sounds silly and dramatic, but there are thousands of such foolhardy reactions recorded on emotionally critical days. You may have been planning to go out for the evening and looking forward to it all day, but if your partner delays or criticises you in some way, no matter how well-meaning that may be, you are liable to overreact. You may sulk, refuse to go or start a row quite unintentionally.

If something goes wrong with the normal routine at work, you could become exasperated: ranting and raving may put you outside the front door permanently. Or, perhaps, you could use your authority and dismiss a subordinate for a mere triviality which, in your present mood, appears to be a heinous offence.

The Negative Phase

As this cycle switches to the negative stage, you become less co-operative generally. You become moody, easily depressed, touchy and sensitive to issues that ordinarily do not bother you much. You suddenly feel the world owes you a living and that everyone is against you. The most marked effect is felt by those who have to work with you, or by your loved ones.

However, there is another manifestation to this negative phase of the emotional cycle. You become a demon shopper, finding fault with everyone and everything from the poor shop assistant to the shop decor. You may check your change so deliberately that you insult the intelligence (and the feelings) of the cashier and, in extreme cases, it is possible to be barred from certain stores as a result of your behaviour.

Oddly enough, you may be unaware of your extreme behaviour. On day 22, the nadir of the cycle, everything and everyone is your enemy: you have a totally negative outlook and your moods may be extreme. As this rhythm slowly moves towards the next critical day, however, life begins to take on a better perspective. At this switch-over day you are liable to exhibit humour that can be questionable. Overconfidence could play a part, too: you may take on responsibilities you do not really want.

Generally speaking, while the normal change-over period for the physical cycle is around 24 hours, at least 48 hours should be allowed for the emotional rhythm. This will allow a clear period of time to avoid any possible lapses of behaviour.

Driving should be avoided if it is at all possible because, when pessimism prevails, the danger of accidents looms rather large. Putting yourself into stressful situations does not help matters either.

Of course, most of us are committed to certain courses of action or behaviour because of our occupation or other circumstances, and we are not able to 'shut up shop' for such a long time on a regular basis. Yet in some countries this is more or less exactly what does happen. Drivers are asked to work indoors for the duration of critical days or, if allowed to drive, are asked to display a little flag that shows the rest of the world their biorhythmic state. In some Japanese cities, where the study of biorhythms is almost a way of life, taxi drivers show almost fanatical enthusiasm for the subject, and it is now a common sight for these little flags to be seen flying from vehicles.

The Question of Free Will

So the cycle continues, moving into the positive stage once more, and, with the accent on sensitivity, it is obviously wise to take the trouble to chart your emotional rhythm. Even if nothing happens, and may not for years, it is a reliable guide for avoiding the possibilities of emotional conflict. Equally, however, it must not be accepted that because you are to about to experience a critical day you must do this or that. Arguments are often used to prove that scientific behavioural predictions are impossible. How can we attempt to explain something that, first and foremost, is subject to free will?

We tend to choose our own way of life, usually to conform with our surroundings – but not always. At the least, non-conformity can be said to account for business geniuses, con-men, creative artists, heroes and heroines. All of us have free will to choose our actions, but the vast majority of us conform by finding the most comfortable niche in society and staying there, only rarely straying from it when we feel the urge to do so, or by invitation.

However, in our defence of this we are often at our most vulnerable. When we couple social conformity with the result of research into behavioural patterns, we all fit in somewhere. Some will stay 'out in the cold' a little longer than others but, eventually, they too will return to the fold to be counted.

In competitive events of all kinds, the most natural thing is to want to win and the nature of the winning reflects the behaviour of the individual. There is the out-and-out competitor who has to win at all costs and employs all the skills at hand to do so. At the other end of the line we have the rank outsider, who has no chance. The emotional rhythm in the positive phase can help both contenders. Both may have equal chances at the starting line, but it is performance that counts.

Entertainers perform better when their rhythms are in the plus stage. Small personal nuances are expressed far more effectively, which is particularly important to comedians when practising their special talents.

Using the Positive Stage

Engaging in teamwork of any kind requires a certain amount of acting ability, particularly if personal preferences have to be put to one side to concentrate on the issues at hand. Whether involved in sporting events, crime detection, selling, advertising, marketing or simply being part of a team in an office, a certain amount of sublimation of natural desires and preferences has to be exercised for successful results to be achieved. This is best done when the emotional rhythm is in the positive phase. Even television newsreaders or programme presenters are less likely to fluff their lines at such a time.

If you are thinking of proposing to your love, you might be forgiven for first establishing your mutual biorhythm status. You could be in for a big surprise. It is found that married partners are often at total variance in their respective rhythms; this will be dealt with more fully in Chapter 6, on compatibilities. If you are the one doing the asking, make sure that you are in the positive stage at least. You will be better able to cope with the results of your proposal.

When planning large-scale business matters, do so in the positive stage of the emotional rhythm. This will enable you to convey your personal enthusiasm to others, to be on the ball and be able to cope well in question and answer sessions.

Even if your physical cycle is down, you can still take part in a wide range of sports, and enjoy the experience if in a plus phase of the emotional cycle. All you have to do is remember your physical ability for the day in question and do not overdo it.

Allowing for the Negative Phase

When emotionally under par in the negative stage, there is still no reason why you should not take part in any kind of activity, provided you allow for your limitations as indicated by your own biorhythm chart. In the approximate 48-hour period of a critical day, however, taking part in sports which include an element of danger or which need split-second timing is not recommended. Stock-car racing, motor sports, motorcycle events, horse trials and similar activities should be avoided if at all possible, as you are more likely to be prone to error. Of course, if you wish to risk serious accident, that is your affair, but remember that in competitive sports you may take someone else with you, or be responsible for the demise of others because of your inability to cope with certain situations.

Biorhythmic Pre-knowledge of Others

Biorhythms will not predict the outcome of any event, of course, but they will indicate the potential you have for any given day. How you use this information to dictate your subsequent actions is entirely up to you.

The advantage of biorhythmic pre-knowledge is that it not only indicates your particular disposition for that day, but must do so for everyone else too. This is an unprecedented gift to the astute in the sales and promotion business.

I know of one sales manager who had biorhythm charts prepared for his entire sales force and his biggest buyers. A little judicial juggling here, some careful timing there, and the sales graph went soaring sky-high. It must be to your advantage to be aware of another person's weakness and capitalise on it. This is not an unfair advantage; it is using biorhythms in an intelligent manner to get a little more out of life – and it is open to everyone else to do the same!

If you suffer from high blood pressure, you will want to avoid deliberately taking risks on an emotionally critical day. If you are sensible, you are likely to curb your tongue if a slip could easily affect business relationships in important policy matters. You should concentrate on routine matters and tidy up loose ends at those times when you know that substantial concentration on the more important matters is not so easy.

Good Timing and Good Sense

If you lack perception at the best of times, you could improve your performance by more than 50 per cent if you learned to time your affairs so that they nearly always favour you. Take the annual Christmas party. It often shows people at their worst. If you are easily embarrassed and it is not going to be a good day for socialising, you have two choices: make a reasonable excuse and do not go, though this may be wrongly misinterpreted by your colleagues and boss; or attend but keep a low profile and slip away at the earliest opportunity.

The sudden freedom involved in such situations, before alcohol adds to the confusion, will bring together people exhibiting almost perfect biorhythmic responses. A check on any individual biorhythm chart would be helpful in these situations, to ensure that all get the best from the event.

Naturally, not everyone's biorhythms will be ideally phased at the same time, but a careful and considerate host will ensure no one gets left out of the fun entirely. We often find that we can get along with certain people even when our biorhythms indicate that we should not be in company at all. Emotional compatibility with others is fully dealt with in Chapter 6, but it is worth noting at this point the times when more caution than usual should be employed.

Sensitivity to atmosphere and people needs very careful handling: often a careless word or deed at the wrong moment can not only prove very embarrassing, but also may stay in the memory for longer than you think. In the negative stage of the emotional rhythm, one is particularly prone to such awkward situations.

The simplest advice is to remember what could happen – and behave accordingly. We are then well on the way to optimum behaviour in our relationships with others. Good behaviour will be noticed by those who matter: you may be singled out for promotion earlier than may be reasonably expected, or required to take on a project they may not ordinarily have thought you could handle.

I have often been struck by the the attitude of interviewers in employment agencies. Sometimes they appear well suited to the job, at others they seem totally out of place. The best times to be on duty could easily be assessed from a simple biorhythmic check, and other tasks easily handled on a temporary basis on inauspicious days. Similarly, a teacher whose biorhythms are not conducive to giving direct instruction could use such periods for setting written work, thus averting a possible loss of face when the class plays up. School discipline improves as a result, for there can be few things worse than a teacher forced into a display of temper or a slanging match with a pupil.

These are just a few of the lessons to be learned from simply keeping a watchful eye on the emotional cycle. Using the three rhythms together improves performance all round, as I shall demonstrate in later chapters. Those who perform well will be noticed, and promotion invariably follows for those who demonstrate ability, especially when it involves human relationships. And none of us can live without others.

4

The Intellectual Cycle

The third cycle controls all our intellectual responses, the powers of reason, perception, judgement, acuity and just plain old-fashioned common sense. The positive phase, which begins with a critical day, accentuates these powers for the good – you shine mentally. Observation is at its peak and simple mental problems are dealt with easily, often without you realising it.

Mentally, you will feel in fine fettle and want to exercise what you may consider to be an under-employed mind. There might be a tendency to make lighthearted calculations from your observations or test your memory with mental games, for the sheer pleasure of flexing the mind.

In fact, a book of puzzles at this stage of your cycle is highly recommended, because if the mind is under-exercised it quickly becomes bored. A highly active intellect left to stagnate for any reason can create social problems. Unintentionally hurtful, cutting, sardonic remarks or justifiable criticisms, which are best left unsaid, can quickly spoil an otherwise good relationship.

The Positive Intellectual Phase

It is doubtful whether we ever use our brains to full capacity, and this rhythm of 33 days, if not correctly understood and properly used, will almost certainly result in the under-employment of a valuable asset.

The more the mind is used, the more it flourishes. It is like the engine of a car: the more it is used correctly, the more efficiently it serves you. Continual short journeys will eventually choke up an engine; a similar result is achieved by the mind under similar circumstances. In the positive phase of this cycle, then, the best thing to do is keep the mind as stimulated as is possible.

Students will find that they will probably learn more in half an hour of study during this phase than they do in a whole day when in the negative stage. Creative pursuits proceed more easily, for ideas flow and perception is at its highest point. The senses are more acute and responses are at a higher level. Debates and discussions go well, conversation flourishes. Because the mind is in such good shape, during the space of an hour or so the amount of subjects covered over after-dinner brandy and coffee will surprise you.

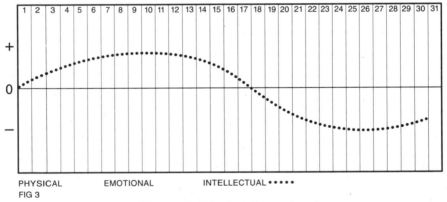

PHYSICAL   EMOTIONAL   INTELLECTUAL • • • •
FIG 3

Figure 3. The intellectual cycle

At this stage of the intellectual cycle, ambitions can receive a boost, especially if you are trying to impress people who matter. You shine at meetings and interviews, successfully displaying your full potential. Your powers of concentration will be at their best: this is a good time to take tests and exams. Planning events will seem easier; small details which may escape your notice under different circumstances are remembered and dealt with – properly.

Money problems beset us all, but if you have to sit down and sort things out, now is the time to do so. Tackling a budget will seem easier – you may even find that more can be put into your savings account than you first thought possible.

This is also the best time to start a new job. All those fresh faces and new routines that have to be mastered will be handled with an expertise you did not think you possessed. Any potentially difficult social problems are considerably eased at this stage of the cycle because the mental processes are working so well that there is sufficient time to remember and deal with details.

Intellectual Critical Days

On a critical day, however, intelligence becomes muddled. You may wake feeling a little fuzzy in the head and, as the day wears on, find that it becomes difficult to express yourself properly.

An intellectual critical day is not one on which to make any important decisions. Judgement and common sense will be impaired and memory can play tricks. Travel could prove a problem, especially if you are on unfamiliar ground, and this would emphasise any possible confusion which you might also experience.

In the intellectual rhythm, a critical day has a slightly longer effect than one in the physical cycle and, as with the emotional rhythm, it would be wise to allow at least 48 hours before you can consider yourself really free of the effects.

Remember, if you have any important meetings scheduled or need to make skilled decisions on or near a critical day, it would be far better to postpone the affair if at all possible. If matters cannot be delayed, remember that you are likely to be prone to error.

You may, of course, feel that nothing is wrong at all. You could sail through an examination and finish early; but you may also find that you forgot or overlooked important points when you go back over your work to check for errors or omissions. Take your time; you may not wish to appear 'slow' in certain types of company but, if you have made a mistake, it is far better to find it before any real damage is done.

If you are a pay clerk, for example, and overpay an employee, it may prove difficult to get the money back, once you have traced the error. If you are held responsible for irregularities in cash dealings, it could cost you more than just money. Your reputation, ability, honesty and integrity may all come under scrutiny, yet all you did was make a simple error that anyone could have made in similar circumstances.

The Negative Phase

In the negative phase of this rhythm, the mental processes slow down, perception becomes dulled, there is a lack of concentration and even the simplest mental tasks seem to need an enormous effort. Sometimes these ups and downs in your mental capacities remain unnoticed from one year to another because they may be very slight.

College lecturers, for example, who are continually flexing their mental muscles may only exhibit slight differences in ability. A fluffed line here, or a short pause there, while their memory seems suddenly faulty, may be all that is apparent. On critical days they may inadvertently address someone by the wrong name or title, or perhaps repeat themselves once or twice.

Sportsmen or sportswomen, however, who live more physical lives and are not called upon to use their minds in the same manner as are professional teachers, may notice their concentration has failed completely.

Curiously, the negative phase of the intellectual cycle does not seem to have a great effect on driving. It appears that most people drive their cars 'automatically', and that emotional reaction is far more deeply involved with this ability than mental acuity. Responses may be dulled a little, but once you have learned to drive, you are inclined to 'absorb' driving techniques physically and emotionally. Mental processes are not used as much as one would suppose. Motorcyclists, however, have to continuously use mental judgement while driving and would be well advised to keep a weather eye on their intellectual rhythms.

It is a generally considered opinion of biorhythm exponents that the second half of the intellectual rhythm, the negative phase, should be used for reviewing work wherever possible. New tasks are better tackled during the cycle's positive stage. Actors and actresses, for example, would find it better to go through their scripts during this period. The mind is less perceptive, it does not want to become involved in new material in the negative phase and is much happier just ticking over. So it is an ideal time for reappraisal, for going over information or material already gathered.

Crime detection often peaks in this phase. The painstaking care with which detectives have to piece together all the evidence is well known. They may get their inspiration during the positive phase, but will find it better to mull over what they already have when in the negative. If they have concluded all of their investigations, it might be better to postpone arresting the prime suspect on an intellectually critical day. If this is not possible, it would be wise to make absolutely sure of the facts before moving in!

We often hear of cases being lost because of a legal technicality in the suspect's favour, so it would be interesting to know if any research has been done on this point. At present, the only information we have is that crime occurs 4.7 per cent more frequently on critical intellectual days than in the positive stage. Serious crimes, such as murder, rape, kidnapping and armed robbery, take place most often when the subject is in the positive phase of the physical cycle, with the other two cycles in negative phase. This appears to be the time when most individuals are particularly capable of great violence. Unfortunately, we can only view crime problems in retrospect: a glance through the records tends to support this theory, although there is insufficient data available to confirm it beyond all reasonable doubt.

Politicians, in particular, have been found to be susceptible to fluctuations in the intellectual rhythm. Constantly in the public eye, they tend to be acutely aware that they are public figures and behave accordingly for the most part. If they are going to make mistakes, however, it is much more likely to be on the critical days of the intellectual rhythm than at any other time. Politics is a mentally orientated way of life and a rather taxing business. Many a politician has well and truly put his or her foot in it when the intellectual cycle has been in an unfavourable phase.

Awareness of Potential

The mini-critical days, at day 9 in the positive phase and day 26 in the negative stage, tend to display the subject's extremes of mental prowess. When in the plus stage, mistakes or over-confidence often occur – almost as if the person has not bothered to prepare for the task in hand. However, brilliant streaks of originality may be shown when in this phase as well. The opposite is true in the negative stage: it almost seems as if the mind cannot cope with any situation. These are extreme examples, of course, but they serve to illustrate the way in which biorhythms can be employed as guidelines for living.

This does not imply that one cannot live without consulting a biogram, nor that accidents will always occur on critical days; accidents can and do occur at other times. However, it is always wise to be fully aware of your strengths and weaknesses before starting any potentially dangerous activities, and try to restrict such undertakings to times when your biorhythms are in favourable conjunction with each other. For instance, you are most likely to survive trouble if your physical and intellectual cycles are positive and your emotional rhythm is negative, than at any other time.

The intellectual cycle is the least studied of the three rhythms, partly because most research into the physical manifestations of biorhythms seems to be connected with the physical and emotional cycles. Nevertheless, the intellectual rhythm should be given the same importance as the other two, because life really is a series of logical – or illogical – steps.

Biorhythms – a Key to Success

Nearly everything you do, if you stop and think seriously about it, is governed by social obligations which, in turn, are based on survival. If you look around, everyone is doing the same things you do. They obey the same impulses and generally observe the same codes of behaviour.

Admittedly, each of us interprets our way of life in our own personal and individual style, and some people stand out more than others, though not necessarily in a better light. There are those who have more or less given up altogether: tramps, down-and-outs and the unfortunates who have suffered some blow to their once-normal lives and have ceased the struggle.

Those who really stand out are those who seize each opportunity as it arises. Many opt for the argument that these people got where they are because their faces fitted or because they had contacts in the right places at the right time and that ability had little to do with their success. This could be quite true up to a point, but some ability got them noticed in the first place – the ability to think, reason and make decisions based on a predetermined course – or they followed their natural desires.

The naturally ambitious will nearly always succeed in using their mental powers to gain the things they most want. The intelligent use of biorhythms could have you up there with them, vying for the same things on equal terms. Naturally, biorhythms cannot give you anything on a plate; that is simply not possible. However, the abilities you do possess can be enhanced by timing opportunities to your best possible advantage. We all want to succeed. Your biorhythms, if used diligently, will help you along the all-important road to success.

5

Calculations

Since biorhythms were first introduced there have been quite a few alternative methods for calculating the various phases, stages and critical days.

These have ranged from specialised calculators that would do the calculations for you in a matter of moments, to having biorhythms charted for you by any one of several organisations. Books have been published that list predetermined codes. All you have to do is look up your personal information in the tables provided.

Six or seven 'dedicated' calculators used to be available, all more or less variations on a theme. Each in their own way produced a reading for the day in question at the touch of a button or two.

You were also able to apply for your personal biograms, which were, and still are, created in widely differing formats; for a very small fee, you can still receive a computer print-out for a month, three months or a year.

Hand-drawn biograms were also created, for a month, three months, six months or a one-year period. In some places this service is still available. You can also apply and have a biogram charted in retrospect for a specific day or period in your own life, or that of a famous or infamous personality from the past.

There was, and still is, no general conformity in the way these are presented. Visually, the easiest style to understand is the generally accepted colour code where the physical cycle is always shown in red, the emotional cycle in blue and the intellectual in green.

Each card is for one calendar month and all the biorhythms are easily and instantly recognised. This means you may go anywhere in the world for any length of time and renew your biogram without too much of a problem.

Today, however, there are many limitations in all these methods because dedicated calculators are no longer available. All the books are more or less out of print, except for a very small handful that have appeared in the last three or four years. The few companies in Great Britain who do advertise a biorhythm charting service may be counted on one hand.

However, the advent of the personal computer has created a whole range of different biorhythm programs that present your personal readings on screen – or as hard copy – at the touch of a button or two and, for the most part, are quite reliable. They may appear on screen as part of the loading/ switch-on program or in a directory as you see fit. The hard copy print-out also varies with different programs.

For personal research purposes I currently hold 15 different programs in a special directory on my own machine. In addition, I have a variety of programs for some of the small hand-held personal computers. Many of these programs and all the calculator systems are, or were, limited to the twentieth century, starting at 1 January 1901 through to 31 December 1999. This makes life rather difficult for students who wish to trace the lives of historical figures.

Establishing the Birth Date

With or without a calculator, it is possible to check in just a few minutes the biorhythms for anyone whose birth date is known. This system may be confidently used for any date from 2 September 1752, when Great Britain decided to adopt the Gregorian Calendar.

Up to that time Britain had used the Julian Calendar and was some 11 days adrift of other countries who had already made the change. Therefore, as a result of the change, 2 September was followed immediately by 14 September. So, any date prior to this may be suspect, and you may need to verify your information for dates before this particular period.

The American colonies changed on this date, for they were still subject to British law, but other countries changed at different times before this and afterwards. Generally speaking, most dates referred to in books and other publications have already been converted to the new system. A few may be quoted in the context of the calendar prevailing at the time in question, but a visit to the local library will furnish you with the necessary details. Students of prominent historical figures and history, who find it fascinating to delve into the pasts of heroes, heroines or villains, may now add the biorhythmic aspect to their investigations. Could biorhythms have had a bearing on the way they acted or thought?

A good biography often lists the full dates of an event so, armed with this and the birth date of the individual concerned, an hour or two may be very profitably and pleasurably passed. Indeed, the compatibility factor between known groups of people may now yield further insight into their relationships.

A few minutes' work will give you similar results for your modern favourites too, whether they be pop stars, actors or sportsmen and sportswomen. Newscasters may fluff their lines several times while you watch: well-known personalities may act in a way not normally associated with them; golfers may appear to be completely off form during a particular match. A host of occasions will offer you food for thought and provide the impetus necessary to check the biorhythms of your favourite personality.

First Steps

The basis of biorhythmic calculation is to determine the number of days that have elapsed from the date of birth up to the date you are interested in (remember to include the date of birth and the date in question in the total). This total is then divided by the number of days duration in each cycle: divide by 23 for the physical cycle, 28 for the emotional and 33 for the intellectual.

In each case the remainder figure will show the stage of the particular rhythm under review. Where there is no remainder, this means that the day following is day 1 of a new positive phase, a critical day, the day on which the cycle starts again.

In the physical rhythm, the positive phase starts on day 1 and lasts until day 12 which is a critical day. Days 2 to 11 are the plus stage which peaks at a mini-critical point on day 7. From day 13 to 23 is the negative stage, with a mini-critical point on day 18.

In the emotional cycle, day 1 starts the positive phase, which lasts until day 15, the critical day, with a mini-critical point on day 8; days 2 to 14 are the plus phase. The negative stage runs from day 16 to day 28 with the mini-critical point occurring on day 22.

The intellectual rhythm starts on day 1 and is positive until the critical day, day 17; the mini-critical day occurs on day 9. The negative stage lasts from day 18 until day 33, with a mini-critical point on day 26.

Determining Biorhythms Without a Calculator

The tables in this section are devised to enable you to calculate biorhythms without a calculator. For our example we will take someone born on 24 May 1950 and calculate their biorhythms for 27 October 1979.

Figure 4 will help you find your total number of days quickly. Where the specific number of years required is not listed, combine the necessary figure to obtain the desired total.

1 × 365 =	365	10 × 365 =	3,650
2 × 365 =	730	20 × 365 =	7,300
3 × 365 =	1,095	30 × 365 =	10,950
4 × 365 =	1,460	40 × 365 =	14,600
5 × 365 =	1,825	50 × 365 =	18,250
6 × 365 =	2,190	60 × 365 =	21,900
7 × 365 =	2,555	70 × 365 =	25,550
8 × 365 =	2,920	80 × 365 =	29,200
9 × 365 =	3,285	90 × 365 =	32,850

Figure 4. Day/year calculations from 1–90 years

Figure 5 (below) shows the number of each day throughout the year, calculated progressively.

Day	Jan	Feb	Mar	Apr	May	Jun	Jul	Aug	Sep	Oct	Nov	Dec
1	1	32	60	91	121	152	182	213	244	274	305	335
2	2	33	61	92	122	153	183	214	245	275	306	336
3	3	34	62	93	123	154	184	215	246	276	307	337
4	4	35	63	94	124	155	185	216	247	277	308	338
5	5	36	64	95	125	156	186	217	248	278	309	339
6	6	37	65	96	126	157	187	218	249	279	310	340
7	7	38	66	97	127	158	188	219	250	280	311	341
8	8	39	67	98	128	159	189	220	251	281	312	342
9	9	40	68	99	129	160	190	221	252	282	313	343
10	10	41	69	100	130	161	191	222	253	283	314	344
11	11	42	70	101	131	162	192	223	254	284	315	345
12	12	43	71	102	132	163	193	224	255	285	316	346
13	13	44	72	103	133	164	194	225	256	286	317	347
14	14	45	73	104	134	165	195	226	257	287	318	348
15	15	46	74	105	135	166	196	227	258	288	319	349
16	16	47	75	106	136	167	197	228	259	289	320	350
17	17	48	76	107	137	168	198	229	260	290	321	351
18	18	49	77	108	138	169	199	230	261	291	322	352
19	19	50	78	109	139	170	200	231	262	292	323	353
20	20	51	79	110	140	171	201	232	263	293	324	354
21	21	52	80	111	141	172	202	233	264	294	325	355
22	22	53	81	112	142	173	203	234	265	295	326	356
23	23	54	82	113	143	174	204	235	266	296	327	357
24	24	55	83	114	144	175	205	236	267	297	328	358
25	25	56	84	115	145	176	206	237	268	298	329	359
26	26	57	85	116	146	177	207	238	269	299	330	360
27	27	58	86	117	147	178	208	239	270	300	331	361
28	28	59	87	118	148	179	209	240	271	301	332	362
29	29		88	119	149	180	210	241	272	302	333	363
30	30		89	120	150	181	211	242	273	303	334	364
31	31		90		151		212	243		304		365

Figure 5. Number of days throughout the year

Figure 6 (below) shows which years are leap years, which of course you must allow for in your calculations.

1756	1760	1764	1768	1772	1776	1780	1784	1788
1792	1796	1804	1808	1812	1816	1820	1824	1828
1832	1836	1840	1844	1848	1852	1856	1860	1864
1868	1872	1876	1880	1884	1888	1892	1896	1904
1908	1912	1916	1920	1924	1928	1932	1936	1940
1944	1948	1952	1956	1960	1964	1968	1972	1976
1980	1984	1988	1992	1996	2000	2004	2008	2012

Figure 6. Leap years 1752–2012
(NB: The years 1800 and 1900 were *not* leap years)

In our example, on 27 October, our subject would have been 29 years old plus the extra days. Therefore, from Figure 4, we will begin our calculations.

$$20 \times 365 = 7,300$$
$$+ \ 9 \times 365 = \underline{3,285}$$
$$\overline{10,585} \text{ days}$$

From Figure 6 we see the subject has lived through seven leap years. Add these to the total, thus:

$$7$$
$$+ \ 10,585$$
$$\overline{10,592} \text{ days}$$

We now need to know how many days have elapsed since the birth date, 24 May 1950, until 27 October 1979. From figure 5 we see that 27 October is day 300 and that 24 May is day 144, therefore:

$$300$$
$$- \ 144$$
$$\overline{156}$$

Bring forward 10,592 and add this to 156 to obtain the next figure required:

$$
\begin{array}{r}
10,592 \\
+\quad 156 \\
\hline
10,748
\end{array}
$$

You must now add 1 to this figure for the day in question, thus:

$$
\begin{array}{r}
1 \\
+\ 10,748 \\
\hline
10,749
\end{array}
$$

Our subject has, therefore, lived a total of 10,749 days, inclusive of the day for which we wish to calculate the biorhythms.

To determine the physical rhythm, we now divide this by 23. The whole figure represents the number of full cycles experienced; the remainder figure indicates the stage of the current cycle. Thus:

$$
23 \overline{)10,749} \quad 467 \text{ remainder } 8
$$

Therefore, on 27 October the physical rhythm is 8 days into the plus stage.

Similarly, for the emotional rhythm we now divide our total of 10,749 by 28.

$$
28 \overline{)10,749} \quad 383 \text{ remainder } 25
$$

On 27 October the emotional rhythm has reached day 25 of its cycle and is in the negative stage.

Again, for the intellectual cycle we divide 10,749 by 33:

$$
33 \overline{)10,749} \quad 325 \text{ remainder } 24
$$

Therefore, on 27 October the intellectual rhythm is at day 24, in its negative phase.

So, in our example, the full biorhythmic reading for the day is: physical cycle, 8; emotional cycle, 25; intellectual cycle, 24.

The interpretation for this biorhythmic stage would be: this is an ideal day for clearing up anything which requires a certain amount of physical participation but not too much mental concentration. Mull over a few minor problems, do a little spring cleaning or take the dog for a walk.

Determining Biorhythms Using a Calculator

In order to eliminate the mathematical drudgery and reduce any possibility of error, take an ordinary calculator and work out the number of days which have elapsed from the date of birth to the date in question, using the tables as before.

It is most important to remember to add one day to your total to account for the day under review. Using the same example as you did earlier, your total will be 10,749.

Using your calculator, divide this number by 23, 28 and 33 respectively.

$$10,749 \div 23 = 467.34782 \text{ (physical cycle)}$$

$$10,749 \div 28 = 383.89285 \text{ (emotional cycle)}$$

$$10,749 \div 33 = 325.72727 \text{ (intellectual cycle)}$$

For the physical biorhythm stage, multiply the decimal remainder by 23, thus: $0.34782 \times 23 = 7.99986$. To the nearest whole number this is 8.

For the emotional biorhythm stage, multiply the decimal remainder by 28, thus: $0.89285 \times 28 = 24.9998$. To the nearest whole number this is 25.

For the intellectual biorhythm stage, multiply the decimal remainder by 33, thus: $0.72727 \times 33 = 23.99991$. To the nearest whole number this is 24.

Once you have calculated the figures of these cycles for one particular date, it is a simple matter to make up a biogram for a month, or for as long as you like.

Whether you want to go back in time to see why your performance was impaired or better than average, or whether you want to make up a card for a month in advance, this will provide you with two very simple methods of producing charts without the aid of a specialised biorhythmic calculator.

All the information you need to calculate and use biorhythms has been provided in this book, and there are a number of blank charts at the back for you to experiment with (see pages 138–9). All you need, therefore, is three coloured pens or pencils (it is best to stick to the accepted colour codes for the cycles – red for physical, blue for emotional and green for intellectual), and a protractor to complete the curves. Work out your calculations for the first day of the month in order to arrive at the starting figures in each of the three cycles. It will be easier to pick out the critical days, draw the curves between the points and complete the rest of the month accordingly.

Do check carefully to ensure that you have got everything right; with practice it will soon fall into place. Here is another example to help you get into the swing of things; this time we will assume we want the biorhythms for 31 December 1999 for someone born on 24 June 1939.

On 31 December 1999 our subject would be 60 years old: thus, the whole calculation is:

60×365 + leap year days + days from 24 June + 1.

$60 \times 365 = 21,900$ (see Figure 4).

Leap years from 1939 until 1999 = 15 (see Figure 6).

Thus:
$$
\begin{array}{r}
21,900 \\
+ \quad 15 \\
\hline
21,915
\end{array}
$$

From Figure 5 we find that 31 December is 365 and 24 June is 175. Therefore:
$$
\begin{array}{r}
365 \\
- \quad 175 \\
\hline
190
\end{array}
$$

Thus:
$$
\begin{array}{r}
190 \\
+ \, 21,915 \\
\hline
22,105 \\
+ \qquad 1 \text{ (for the day in question)} \\
\hline
22,106
\end{array}
$$

We now divide this total figure by the relative cycle lengths: 23 for the physical rhythm, 28 for the emotional and 33 for the intellectual. We will do this first without a calculator.

Physical:

$$23\overline{)22{,}106} \quad 961 \text{ remainder } 3$$

Emotional:

$$28\overline{)22{,}106} \quad 789 \text{ remainder } 14$$

Intellectual:

$$33\overline{)22{,}106} \quad 669 \text{ remainder } 29$$

The biorhythms for this day in question are, therefore: physical cycle, day 3; emotional cycle, day 14; intellectual cycle, day 29.

When we use a pocket calculator we use the figure of 22,106, the number of days elapsed since the birth date to the day under review, and divide this total by the appropriate cycle lengths.

$$22{,}106 \div 23 = 961.13043 \text{ (physical cycle)}$$

$$22{,}106 \div 28 = 789.5 \qquad \text{(emotional cycle)}$$

$$22{,}106 \div 33 = 669.87878 \text{ (intellectual cycle)}$$

Now multiply the decimal remainder by the cycle length involved:

Physical: $0.13043 \times 23 = 2.99989$ (3 to the nearest whole number)

Emotional: $0.5 \times 28 = 14$ (straightforward result)

Intellectual: $0.87878 \times 33 = 28.99974$ (29 to the nearest whole number)

The biorhythms for the day are, therefore: physical cycle, day 3; emotional cycle, day 14; intellectual cycle, day 29.

Biorhythmically, this could be interpreted as feeling fairly good physically, but emotionally a little restless. Your judgement, however, will be suspect. It might be better to let the day pass as it will, rely on your natural sixth sense or work on first impressions. Defer important decisions, if possible.

Once you have had a few practice runs, it should be fairly easy to work out these calculations for yourself. Practise with friends and relatives or anyone else who attracts your interest.

In Chapter 10 (see page 129) you will find the birth dates of over 300 well-known people from all walks of life: from history, sport, politics, entertainment, and individuals who, by their actions, thoughts or words, have made a niche for themselves in the pages of history.

As long as you remember that biorhythms do not in themselves have a cause and effect, but are subject to prevailing conditions, you will find that their stage and phase may have had a bearing on why some individuals behaved in a certain manner on a particular occasion. For example, it is often a source of surprise to discover the basis of a famous, or infamous, partnership – biorhythmically speaking.

However, as far as you are concerned – and that is what this book is all about – you now know how to live with your biorhythms in order to experience a more satisfactory way of life, in every sense of the word.

6

Compatibility

W e all want to get along as best we can with those around us, but this can sometimes be an uncertain process. We may find ourselves behaving slightly irrationally towards someone we have just met for the first time: something does not quite seem to 'click' into place. In effect, our relationship does not get off to a very good start and, as time goes by, we find that there is something about the association that prevents it from really getting off the ground, no matter how hard we try.

At other times, with other people, an immediate rapport is established. We find that we think alike and can generally have a good time in each other's company.

By comparing our biorhythm charts we might find the reason for these apparent discrepancies in our relationships. After all, it is a logical step to propose that what biorhythms do for us, they must do for others.

Reactions to personal biorhythms can and do vary from individual to individual, of course. Yet they can provide guidelines as to how we may most successfully relate to others, and the system used for comparisons is easy to follow.

If you look at Figures 7 and 8 on page 70, you will immediately observe the similarity between them. Both have intellectual critical days on the 4th and 20th of the month. Subject A has physical critical days on the 8th and 20th, B on the 7th and 19th. Their emotional critical days differ a little more. Subject A's are on the 3rd and 17th, while B's occur on the 12th and 26th.

Their intellectual rhythms are exactly in phase but they are one day apart in their physical rhythms and nine days apart in their emotional cycles.

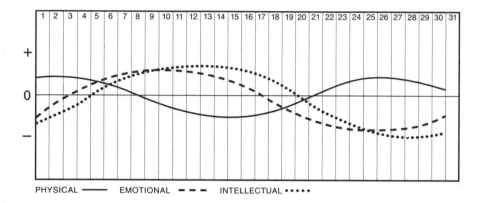

PHYSICAL ——— EMOTIONAL ▬ ▬ ▬ INTELLECTUAL •••••

Figure 7. Subject A

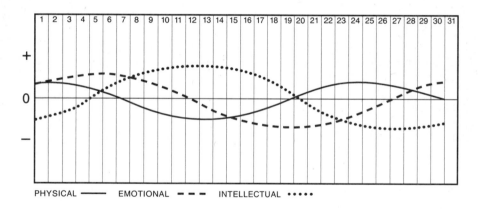

PHYSICAL ——— EMOTIONAL ▬ ▬ ▬ INTELLECTUAL •••••

Figure 8. Subject B

In such a case, it is reasonable to suppose that these two people will think and act alike, but that there might be a slight difference in their emotional approach to life. In fact, they are very good friends. They hit it off the day they met and the relationship has gone from strength to strength ever since.

The subjects of figures 9 and 10 – we will call them C and D – are quite different. They both have emotional critical days on the same day, but their cycles are in opposing stages.

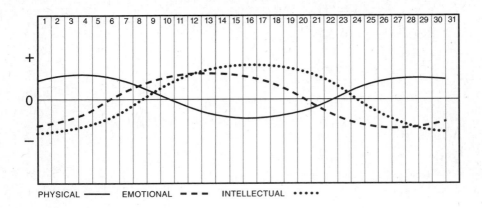

PHYSICAL ——— EMOTIONAL – – – INTELLECTUAL •••••

Figure 9. Subject C

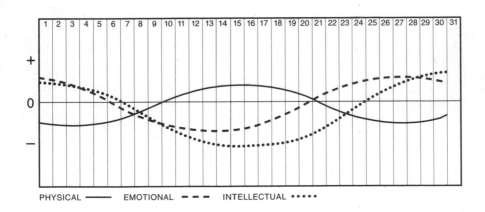

PHYSICAL ——— EMOTIONAL – – – INTELLECTUAL •••••

Figure 10. Subject D

Subject C's positive stage runs from the 6th to the 20th, but D goes into the negative stage on the 6th and switches again to the positive phase on the 20th.

C has a physical critical day going into the negative phase

on the 10th and the positive critical day on the 22nd. D's cycle is the reverse of this: this rhythm turns positive on the 10th and swings into the negative phase on the 21st.

Intellectually, their biorhythms are one day apart. C experiences the first critical day on the 8th and switches to the negative on the 24th. D moves into the negative on the 7th and changes back to the positive on the 24th.

Compatibility Ratings

In biorhythmic terms, A and B have a total compatibility assessment of 85 per cent, which is unusually high. This is made up of 91 per cent physical compatibility, 64 per cent emotional and 100 per cent intellectual.

The total rating for C and D, on the other hand, is only 7 per cent, made up of 4 per cent physical compatibility, nil per cent emotional and 3 per cent intellectual – exceptionally low figures.

These charts are taken from life and are of four people who have to get along with each other. While A and B are just good friends, C and D have to work with each other. Before C and D were aware of their compatibility rating, there was a definite feeling of antipathy between them. Now that they are aware of a possible reason for this feeling, they tend to get along far better than they did originally, although their basic personality differences are still apparent. They have learned to get along with each other by making simple adjustments to their own personality traits while, at the same time, recognising the problems that may arise between them.

An easy method of assessing compatibility is to calculate the difference between the individual cycles in days, each day representing a proportional difference in the cycles. These calculations are made for each rhythm individually, then added together to give an overall figure. If this total is then divided by three – the number of cycles involved – the resultant figure represents the overall compatibility rating.

It is very important to remember that this compatibility factor stays constant, irrespective of what the individual reading for any day may be.

When we look at at Figures 11 and 12 (below), we see that on the 1st of the month subject E is on the 4th day of their physical rhythm and F on their 8th day, a difference of four days. If we look at the chart of compatibility percentages on page 75, we will see that four days apart represents 65 per cent. On the 2nd day E's rhythm will be on day 5 and F's on day 9: still four days apart.

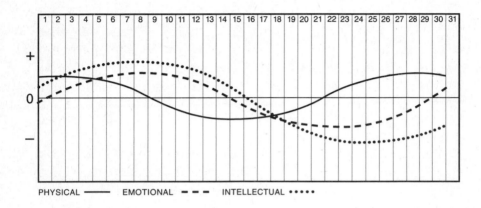

Figure 11. Subject E

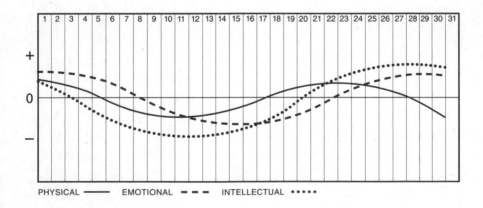

Figure 12. Subject F

In the emotional rhythm, E is on day 1 on the 1st day of the month and F is on day 8, the difference being seven days or 50 per cent. The following day their individual stages will have increased by one more day, but the compatibility factor remains at 50 per cent.

If we now look at the intellectual rhythm, we see that E is on day 2 and F is on day 15 on the 1st day of the month, which represents only a 9 per cent compatibility factor.

When we add these three factors together, 65 per cent for the physical, 50 per cent for the emotional and 9 per cent for the intellectual, we arrive at a gross figure of 124. When we divide this total by three – the number of rhythms – we arrive at an overall assessment figure of 41 per cent, to the nearest whole number. This overall figure also remains constant.

Key Factors

It is at this point that there is a difference of opinion between biorhythm experts. Some feel this figure should be treated as a guide only; others think it is a reliable pointer when it comes to assessing compatibility.

Either way, it has been observed that the cycle which shows the highest percentage in the total will feature most strongly in the relationship. Thus, between A and B the figures were 91 per cent (physical), 64 per cent (emotional) and 100 per cent (intellectual). The highest figure, therefore, is in the intellectual cycle.

The relationship between these two people is accentuated by their almost uncanny ability to read each other's minds when working things out. They both have the same basic approach to life and display similar feelings on a wide variety of subjects. They also express similar emotional ideals.

In the case of C and D, it is a completely different story. The totals are 4 per cent for the physical cycle, nil per cent for the emotional and 3 per cent for the intellectual: this is not a lot to work with when trying to assess the overall key factor in this relationship because the figures are so small and close. In fact, there is no key factor; these two people simply have absolutely nothing in common.

Days apart in cycle	Physical cycle %	Emotional cycle %	Intellectual cycle %
0	100	100	100
1	91	93	94
2	83	86	88
3	74	79	82
4	65	71	76
5	57	64	70
6	48	57	64
7	39	50	58
8	30	43	52
9	22	36	46
10	13	29	39
11	4	21	33
12	4	14	27
13	13	7	21
14	22	0	15
15	30	7	9
16	39	14	3
17	48	21	3
18	57	29	9
19	65	36	15
20	74	43	21
21	83	50	27
22	91	57	33
23	100	64	39
24		71	46
25		79	52
26		86	58
27		93	64
28		100	70
29			76
30			82
31			88
32			94
33			100

Figure 13. Compatibility table
(All figures are quoted to the nearest whole number)

Any number of people can be assessed in a compatibility exercise and any day can be assessed for the best time for an activity. To check overall compatibility, first establish how many days apart your subjects' biorhythms are. Then use Figure 13 (see page 75) to find their percentage compatibility figures for each cycle. Add these together and divide the total by 3 to arrive at the overall compatibility figure.

Partnerships

The higher the compatibility factor in the physical rhythms of two people, the more readily you will tackle those tasks requiring physical effort to be undertaken in unison.

Sports and recreational activities need both parties to act more or less harmoniously for them to be enjoyed to the full. If you put two people in a canoe and send them off downriver, or put two people at the bottom of a mountain to climb, it is not going to be very pleasant for one if the other cannot or will not share the physical burden.

The more out of step the biorhythms, the greater the compensatory approach needed, because some sort of harmony must be struck if those involved are to have a good time. Compromises at an early stage will go a long way to achieving a all-round worthwhile day. One of the partners may be in the positive phase of the physical cycle when the other is nearing the end, on a critical day, in the negative phase or just beginning the physical cycle. In such a case, the former must be allowed to take the lead with the other bringing up the rear as best they can in the prevailing circumstances. Provided that each allows for the difference in phase and understands how this will affect their individual performance the day should go well.

Group Compatibility

Compatibility does not stop at just two people; ratings between three, four or indeed any number of people can be worked out and used to achieve more successful relationships. This assessment allows all concerned to maximise their available potential. Their thinking, therefore, must also become more positive, with improved results all round.

For example, when we look at the problems that confront modern football team managers when selecting their players for the Saturday match, the intelligent use of biorhythms could go a long way to help them use the best possible players at their time of maximum potential.

The first reaction is to choose 11 players who are at the peak of their performance as far as their biorhythms are concerned, but this would not necessarily achieve the best results. A reasonable amount of non-compatibility must exist between any group of people for a variety of reasons. Most clubs have far more players than is generally appreciated; they have to allow for substitutes, reserve teams and trainees, and will have certain standards to maintain. So, the first step is to see how each individual gets along with the others, on and off the field. The compatibility between the players and the manager should also be checked.

Having done this, the next step is to select from the club's star players as far as possible. In the unlikely event that they all get along with each other perfectly, the selection of the best possible team, biorhythmically, would be easy, of course. Yet it would still be inadvisable to select all those players at the peak of their biorhythmic positive stages, for then there would be less of a 'team' performance: all of the players would feel fully capable of winning by their own efforts. Far and away the most effective selection should be on the basis of the positive physical stage for each player with, where possible, the best compatibility rating between them and an allowance for any substitutes.

Unless there was a marked degree of emotional incompatibility between them, the team's emotional phasing need not necessarily be high or even in the positive stage, for there would be a greater inclination towards sharing the game at other stages. Intellectually, all that is needed is concentration, irrespective of the cycle's phasing. So, if all the players were at absolute peak biorhythmic performance in each of the cycles, they would most likely lose the match because of their inability to perform successfully as a team.

Cricket, however, calls for a different set of skills and would need a different approach towards the selection of a successful side. Each of the batting team has to have a steady eye and, therefore, needs to be in the intellectual plus phase. They also require the physical ability to make strokes that score, so their physical rhythms would need to be auspicious.

Bowlers need to be perfectly attuned, so their emotional rhythms would need to be good and, of course, they need to deliver balls consistently accurately and powerfully, so physical rhythms would also need to be considered.

Tennis requires stamina, vigour and concentration, so all three rhythms should be in their positive phase for a successful game. However, the emphasis is on accuracy so both the emotional and the physical rhythms become additionally important.

As with all professional sports, once the techniques have been mastered, play becomes almost second nature. The emphasis, therefore, is placed on the emotional and physical rhythms being in positive phase for successful participation.

In a department store, numerous people have to get along with each other and with customers under fairly restrictive conditions. Obviously, it is not a practicable exercise to try to verify the biorhythmic conditions of such a large number of people. Nevertheless, the staff could benefit from knowing their personal rhythms and individual compatibility potential. So, apart from their selling techniques, some of the individual sales staff who experience friction in certain relationships might find their selling ability limited as a result.

Working Relationships

Poor working relationships can often stem from unsuitable management. Irrespective of any banding together of junior staff against an oppressive superior, the potential for a good (or bad) working atmosphere can be assessed by setting all the employees' compatibility ratings (see Figure 13 on page 75) in a chart such as that shown in Figure 14 (see page 79).

In this example, A is the departmental manager, supervising six members of staff, B, C, D, E, F and G. You can see that A gets on fairly well with two of his staff (C and E) but not so well with the others. The six staff, in turn, all get on well with each other, with the exception of G. Higher management solved this problem by transferring A to another department to head a different sales team with whom he was more compatible. They put in a new head of sales in the original department, which resulted in a happier group and much improved sales performance all round.

A						
15	B					
64	91	C				
47	85	79	D			
70	86	89	92	E		
30	100	94	86	80	F	
10	18	24	12	15	33	G

Figure 14. Assessing working relationships

One other improvement that could have been made was to have put G, the odd man out in this original group, into another section. If they had done so, it may have proved mutually beneficial for all concerned, for G just could not get along with anyone.

Translate this sort of problem into a factory environment and the inherent dangers soon become apparent. Conveyor-belt production techniques are monotonous and can lead to boredom and irritation, frequently resulting in accidents. In some workplaces, employees may have to share machinery for short periods. Incompatibility and a need for bursts of absolute concentration can lead to accidents. When accident rates rise, so do insurance costs – and the tempers of management. Returning to Figure 14 (see page 79), if G was the supervisor in such an environment, the turnover of staff would probably be very high indeed.

Among library staff it has been found that, although almost everyone gets along in their intellectual phasing, their emotional and physical assessment ratings are uncommonly poor. This is a good example of working conditions attracting people who have the ability to do a specific type of job, but not necessarily the ability to get along with each other.

The incident rate of incompatibility is often inordinately high in a word-processing section staffed by very young workers. Their supervisor must, therefore, exercise discipline combined with understanding. Physical compatibility is not really of great importance here, but emotionally and intellectually there is a need to use great discretion. This could be achieved by allotting certain types of work only to those who show the aptitude for those specific tasks.

Of course, this may create other problems, but as long as staff are given an adequate explanation, the biorhythmic compatibility assessment of all the employees involved can only help to improve their output.

Improving Relationships

On the whole, most people will try to improve their relationships with others if explanations and guidelines are offered. You may not really understand why you have never got along with one person but have always got along another, but you are probably willing to try and improve a poor relationship even if there is no guarantee of success.

Biorhythms may reveal a potential solution to the problem, but it should be remembered that compatibility is subject to personal behavioural patterns and the prevailing conditions of the moment. The percentage figures are constant and, for the best results, personal biorhythm charts should be calculated so that mutually advantageous times for joint activities can be arranged.

The overall assessment figures ought really to be regarded as a guide only; the individual cycle figures are the most important.

Physical Percentages

When assessing the physical rating, 100 per cent is fine for all activities requiring joint participation. A figure of around 75 per cent needs the temporarily stronger partner to allow for the weaker partner's inability to be as active. A rating of 50 per cent or less indicates that the difference requires the good judgement of both partners to time events for mutual satisfaction. That can only lead to a better understanding and a more rewarding relationship.

Where several people are concerned, greater allowances need to be made. With a group of four or more, at least one member is likely to be present purely for the sake of the activity involved. For example, three fanatics and one player along for the ride might find it difficult to enjoy a round of golf.

Emotional Percentages

In the emotional cycle, a 100 per cent rating is fine for most associations except for long-term or close partnerships such as marriage or family relationships where too-similar rhythms can lead to tension. In very close relationships, having the same ups and downs and the same critical days can be boring and is liable to cause almost as many problems as completely incompatible emotional rhythms.

Too little stimulation can make a relationship stagnate and, if both partners are in a bad mood on a negative critical day, then heaven help them and those around them! From 45 to 65 per cent is about the best rating for married couples; the difference will provide a constant stimulus because their rhythms will be slightly out of phase all the time.

When the emotional assessment figure is below 40 per cent, it is regarded as poor. Both partners will need tact, good timing and understanding in any situation requiring emotional rapport. A careful study of their individual charts will reveal the best time to stage such activities. In these cases the couple's sex life tends to remain quite stimulating.

Intellectual Percentages

A 100 per cent rating of the intellectual biorhythm will produce the best results in all types of relationships, although a lack of stimulation could be experienced because the parties think alike. Around 75 per cent is a good figure, because then one partner is always able to complement the other when their cycles are at variance. The higher level of perception of the one partner will offset the under-par thinking and reasoning of the other. A figure of about 50 per cent or lower shows a contrasting intellectual approach, requiring tact and diplomacy that at times could stretch forbearance.

If both partners allow for the difference in their levels of perception and, again, use their personal charts to time their best moments for all-important joint decisions, problems can be avoided.

The higher the overall compatibility rating, the better any kind of relationship is likely to be, although it may be coloured by the rhythm with the highest percentage. For example, if the physical rating is the highest, it probably means that the relationship is based on both partners' ability to enjoy each other's physical presence. If the highest rating is on the emotional level, it means the partners are temperamentally suited; if the intellectual rating is the highest, that they are mentally attuned.

Knowing the Good and the Bad

When starting a business relationship with a friend, it would be wise to check your compatibility rating. If it is intellectually high but low on the other two, do not let it worry you too much. Work on the weak points in the association and your business projects should prosper. Even if the assessment figures are poor all round, it does not mean that you cannot succeed. You will just have to work a little bit harder at maintaining the status quo in those areas where you are at widest variance.

Young couples considering marriage may well be a little dismayed by a poor emotional assessment but, as has already been shown, this has proved to be an almost standard result in successful, long-term associations and marriages.

Consider the teacher/pupil, driver/conductor, doctor/ nurse relationship, and that of nurse and patient, if it is a long-term arrangement where the patient may be looked after by a specialist nurse: all may have their compatibility assessed for a better mutual understanding. As improvements start to show, potential physical, emotional or intellectual problems can be alleviated by long-term planning based on biorhythmic knowledge.

Such insight into your good days and bad must help all your relationships in the long run.

7

The Rhythms of Nature

There is an all-pervading rhythm to life and nature. Rhythms and cycles dominate, not only in the biological study of human beings and our behavioural patterns, or even in the history of the human race, but in practically everything else that we care to investigate.

There are ultradian cycles, that is, rhythms of less than 24 hours' duration, circadian rhythms, those around one day's length, and infradian rhythms, which last a lot longer, as much as a year or more in some cases.

The study of cycles is fascinating and certainly deserves mention here, because such a wide variety of rhythms exist that the average person has probably never really considered them, or perhaps never heard of them; yet they affect us in some way or another almost every day of our lives, whether asleep or awake. In each case I refer here to documented studies: either proven, under strict laboratory conditions or, where possible, observed in the natural state. This book is about human beings and our behavioural patterns, so this is where we will start.

'Night' and 'Morning' People

Apart from sleep patterns which, under normal circumstances, take place once a day, usually at night when all natural diurnal life rests, we show a definite rhythmic pattern in every aspect of our lives.

The human body temperature reaches a peak during waking hours and is at its lowest point when we are asleep. As our temperature rises, so does our efficiency; conversely, we become much less effective as our temperature drops. No two people are exactly alike and we respond to our body rhythms as individuals, not collectively. This why some of us are 'night' or 'morning' people (more popularly, 'owls' or 'larks'). Almost all animals sleep or, more correctly, have to sleep. And we are still not really sure why.

All theories about sleep and its function are largely just that – theories. Perhaps the best reason given to date is that it is time for the body to restore itself after its exertions, wanted or otherwise, while we are awake. Most of us sleep for an average period of anywhere between seven and nine hours a day.

These people tend to live slightly longer than those who disrupt their normal sleep patterns through shiftwork or for other reasons. The latter may experience weaker health and die younger. The other danger for people who experience a loss of sleep is, of course, fatigue, which often leads to accidents.

Those who sleep well seem to worry less and take most things in their stride. Good, sound sleep may have something to do with our learning processes. One thing is certain, however: we need a normal sleep pattern; it must suit us personally, and it must be regular. There is a very strong sleep drive in young adults which lessens or weakens in most of us as we grow older. Elderly people do not need as much sleep as the young; they should allow for this and adjust their days accordingly. However, whatever their personal sleep pattern, at whatever age, they will still be an 'owl' or a 'lark'.

One way of checking which of these two categories applies to you is to take your temperature on the hour every hour until you go to bed, a task that has to be spread over several weeks to be anything like an accurate survey. If you keep a graph of the readings, it is easy to judge your most effective periods, so you can make simple adjustments to your way of life. By timing your maximum efforts to coincide with the periods of the highest readings, you will increase your personal efficiency that much more.

Everyone has a natural eating rhythm, although most people tend to ignore this because of their social or business obligations. It would be better for some people to take in sustenance of some kind every 90 minutes, for instance, while others may benefit more from three main meals a day, with nothing in between.

The constituent parts of any meal affect our efficiency in very different ways. While some of us eat a hearty breakfast with a couple of meals later in the day, others get much more from a light snack first thing, and a heavier meal mid-morning. The composition and timing of such a regimen needs to be adjusted to individual requirements so, if you feel you might benefit from such an experiment, go ahead. You will become more efficient and feel a lot better in yourself. You might also establish a better sleep pattern.

Life Statistics

On average, your heart beats 103,680 times a day and, of course, is a part of another cycle, the vascular system. The heart pumps blood around your body in a never-ending cycle that has detectable variations in much the same way as your sleep cycles, feeding habits or other bodily functions

For as long as your heart continues to beat, you will, on an average day, breathe 24,000 times, drink about 3 pints (1.7 litres) of varying liquids, consume an average 3 lb (1.5 kilos) of food and walk approximately 2 miles (3.5 kilometres), using about 750 muscles in the process.

During this period, you may also say about 4,800 words and, as well as doing all these other things, you will use about 7,000,000 brain cells.

In the meantime your hair will grow about 0.017 inches (0.04 cm), your fingernails about 0.000046 inches, and your toenails some 0.000031 inches. All that in just a 24-hour period!

Our body clock has many other cycles during this one-day period, that can positively stagger those of us who are unaware of how our bodies function.

In this relatively new science of chronobiology, many discoveries have been made about our bodies and the cycles and rhythms to which we are subjected. Irrespective of the biorhythmic behavioural cycles and periods, we can actually plan out a day, and time certain activities, almost to the hour, for best effect.

For example, if out driving at night, our sight is at its weakest point at about 2 a.m. and our lowest ebb altogether is between 4 and 5 a.m. We make the most errors between 3 and 4 a.m., which might make some wonder why so many babies choose to arrive between midnight and 4 a.m.

Men tend to respond more to their sex drive between 7 and 8 a.m. because, while both sexes produce more sex hormones at this hour than at any other time of the day, it does rather depend on whether you are an 'owl' or a 'lark' as to how, or if, you respond to this particular drive!

Despite this, we are at our most creative in the morning between 10 a.m. and 12 noon, and our digestion is at its peak around 1 p.m. We are best at sport between 1 and 2 p.m. and are more adept at dealing with problems between 3 and 4 p.m. After 4 p.m. our bodies tend to perform very well at our 'hobby' sports – cricket, football, jogging, rugby, etc.

Our sense of taste, hearing and smell are much more acute in this period, which is why so many of both sexes prefer to socialise, dine and then make love up to about 10 p.m. – whether an 'owl' or a 'lark'.

Between then and midnight we all slow down a little, some more quickly than others, ready for the sleep period we all know we must have and cannot do without if we are to face the following day. And so on and on …

If married, you will probably make love about 3,000 times in your lifetime. We spend a total of 14 years working, and 20 to 24 years spent in bed is the norm. Travelling takes care of five years; dressing, washing, shaving or applying make-up account for another four, and you will probably spend as long as 70 days just preening yourself and looking in the mirror.

If you are a smoker you may well consume almost a quarter of a ton (over 200 kilos) of tobacco, and the average intake of food in the course of a normal life span is quite staggering. During the equivalent of a total period of six years just spent eating, the average person will consume 6,000 loaves of bread, 10,000 eggs, 4,000 lb (1,800 kilos) of butter and 20,000 lb

(9,000 kilos) of fruit and vegetables. This will be washed down with 20,000 gallons (90,920 litres) of a wide variety of liquids.

Our sweet tooth will dispose of 8,000 lb (3,650 kilos) of sugar while we will eat about 50 head of cattle and some 300 chickens. Shopping for all that food, and other things, will take about three years of waiting in queues.

Not content merely to delve into all our physical idiosyncrasies and all our senses, scientists have made other discoveries in their search for cycles and rhythms.

Occupational Cycles

Loosely using birth dates as the criterion, correlations have been found between certain occupations and cyclic performance. It has been found that musicians, for example, have a better chance of success if born during November, January or February than at any other time. This is not to imply, however, that during the low period, August in this case, there is little chance of becoming successful in this field. Architects flourish better if born during December, May and June; their low point is September or October. Bankers born in August seem to do much better than those born in March. And if you are born during October you have a better-than-average chance of becoming a successful journalist or editor than if you are born in December.

Cyclic performance is noted and logged over such long periods of time that, after a while, it seems that even this occupation may be subject to a rhythm within a rhythm. This is true to such an extent that it is virtually possible to predict certain phenomena with a more than average chance of success. Not only that, but it also appears that other cyclic events are closely linked, even when they share no other relationships that can be detected or determined at the time.

Wheels Within Wheels

It might be difficult to accept that there seems to be a link between police states and temperature fluctuations that, in turn, can affect patterns of style in the art world. Co-operation and the integration of views apparently fall into the same pattern as the phenomena of war, crop improvements and palace intrigues! All these events have been found to operate in a worldwide, 100-year cycle, itself a periodic phenomenon.

While the atmosphere in which we live varies slightly from country to country and from area to area within a country, the surface air pressure at sea level is, on average, about 14.7 pounds per square inch, about one ton per square foot. This pressure is measured by a barometer and recorded as inches of mercury; 14.7 pounds per square inch at sea level equals 29.91 inches of mercury. This barometric pressure is affected by, and changes with, the weather; it can move up or down according to the state of the weather.

A rising barometer is an indication of high pressure on the way; as a rule this is associated with fine dry spells. A falling barometer indicates poor weather: rain, winds and storms. After long years of study, it has been found that barometric pressure has moved in rhythmic cycles of 7.6 years.

Changes of pressure seem to influence human beings and our moods and, in turn, we reflect these moods in many ways. A falling barometer can produce, or is associated with, symptoms of irritability, forgetfulness and restlessness. Regular bouts of sleeplessness are recorded at this time, and all these negative attitudes have been proved to be related to road traffic and industrial accidents; suicides have also been found to occur more in this period. The falling barometer is almost always a sign of some danger, and studies have proved a definite correspondence between human behavioural patterns and weather variations, in both the short and long term.

Over 100-year periods it has been shown that during dry and cold times people tend to rebel in cyclic spells against the accepted order of things. Individualism, race pride and civil wars tend to occur more.

In wet and warm spells, people seem more co-operative, more willing to listen to each other and to become more organised. In dry and warm periods, democracy slowly begins to suffer at all levels, from state control at government level to local social life; personal freedoms tend to decline. There may be more business aggression, but financial confidence tends to decline and there may be economic depression.

In cold and wet periods, there is a gradual decentralisation of government, people need, want and strive for more individualistic self-expression. The more freedom is pursued, however, the more likely the whole balance of things is to collapse once more and anarchy begin to take over before the next weather spell.

It is not quite as straightforward and simplistic as this, but a check on weather conditions during a 100-year period will show how much of what has been described here does occur – and it all happens in almost predetermined cycles.

Local crime occurs in patterns and may be linked with the weather variations. During high summer, in July and August, rape, serious assault and murders peak, more particularly between the hours of 6 p.m. and 6 a.m. Burglary, however, is more likely to occur between the hours of 6 p.m. and 2 a.m. on a Saturday night between late November and the end of February. June sees an upsurge in admissions to mental hospitals, and suicide attempts. Curiously, it is also the month in which more marriages usually take place ...

In the USA between 1920 and 1955, a clearly defined pattern was observed in the construction of residential buildings; this cycle apparently exhibited a 33-month periodicity. What is really fascinating about such cyclic events, however, is why they ever occur in the first place. What is the root cause?

We know very little about our discoveries in these areas, but we do know, for example, that there is a definite cycle, with a length of 9.6 years, governing the abundance of snowshoe rabbits in Canada. The lynx, hawk, owl and marten populations have the same cycle, but we do not know what the cause of the cycle can be.

In the last 300–400 years or so, scientists and researchers have been finding rhythms and cycles galore. Some have been discovered by accident, a few by design. It is possible that we are discovering a lost art or science – we simply do not know. Certain historical patterns repeat themselves, both in the same country and in other parts of the world. The events seem to be closely similar to what has gone before.

Cosmic Cycles

Beyond the bounds of earthly ties are the mysterious forces that govern the constant cyclic nature of the universe. We are able to predict these rhythmic motions with tremendous accuracy, but only hazard guesses as to their cause. We have come to accept that with so much interdependence between these rhythms and cycles, if one should fail, unknown forces can be unleashed.

If, one day, the moon should fail to rise, for instance, would the tide also fail to turn? What would happen if the day's length suddenly altered noticeably? In fact, the length of our day was altered, just perceptibly, about 25 years ago. The real effect, if any, however, will not be noticed for quite a few million years yet.

You may smile and think there is nothing to worry about now, but suppose this is part of a hitherto undiscovered cycle which does have some kind of an effect now. What has caused the recent onset of many weather extremes, the great storms, heatwaves and dry spells that have been occurring all over the world, some in places that have never experienced anything like them in local living or recorded memory? We simply do not know. We can only guess at some of the answers or give part answers – now. In the future, we may find some or all of the answers, and then be ready for the phenomenon next time, if there is a next time. One day, someone is going to find the key. It could be tomorrow, or it may be ten or 100 years from now.

In the meantime, inexplicably, we discover mouse plagues occur in four-year cycles and every commodity price we have studied also fluctuates in cycles. The number of babies born each day occurs in cycles, glaciers are known to melt in cycles; even the amount of cheese we eat fluctuates in cycles.

Synchronicity

One fundamental fact of similar cyclic performances that has come to light is the astonishing synchronicity with which they all tend to interact. All cycles with the same duration peak and trough at the same time. This provides evidence of something that we do not understand at this stage, even if we do appreciate that it can no longer be classified as random behaviour.

There are over 30 widely differing subjects that fall into an eight-year cycle which has been studied over a prolonged period from the mid-1780s to the mid-1960s. In each case they reached their high and low spots at the same time during this period: cigarette production from 1880; lead production from 1821; red squirrel abundance from 1926; pig-iron prices from 1784; sugar prices over a period of more than 200 years; and the growth of pine trees from about 1770. Other cycles are 5.91 years long, some 9.6 years, others 11.2 years in duration.

There are mysterious forces at work. This fairly new study of cycles and rhythms could one day allow us to predict our own potential destiny far more accurately than ever before. It opens new areas of thought with which we may merely play at present. Not that we necessarily understand this new toy we have found; we are not sure that we have just one toy, or even that we have the whole toy. It may only be a part of it, like a single piece of track from a model railway set.

This is an age of discoveries, far more than the early part of the twentieth century was. And the speed with which we are travelling suggests possible answers just around the corner, or the next one, or the next ...

8

Practical Biorhythms

There are few areas where the principles of biorhythms cannot be applied. To do this, you must learn to adapt, stop to reassess what seems to be a doubtful possibility, and you will be able to turn the problem into a positive advantage for yourself. Business people in their offices are as prone to making poor decisions when their biorhythms are in their negative phase as is the third or fourth worker along the conveyor belt on the factory floor. Both will cause problems for those around them if they make errors.

In fact, so much so, that many companies are now taking an active interest in the theory and practice of cyclic performance of employer and employee alike. In every case, improved performance has been recorded, which has led to much increased productivity, which, in turn, has meant better prosperity for all.

Business Efficiency

These days, business efficiency is a high priority for most organisations. In the last 20 to 30 years or so, computers have virtually disposed of the old 'typing pool'. Many managers now have to write their own letters, send faxes or perform other tasks once associated with those once invaluable support staff.

As a result, the timing of events has become absolutely vital. All travel, phone calls and meetings, especially the new inter-company 'network' gatherings using computer links, demand efficient prior management if they are to be successful.

These days, most of us can take all this in our stride. We have to make speedy decisions and we must have plenty of energy in order to display extreme efficiency at managing both our time and that of the people we control.

To succeed in business today, therefore, depends on a very high level of personal performance at all times. There is hardly any let-up. Timing is all-important, so it must be helpful to have not only your own biorhythm chart created for you, but also those of your clients, managers and your own staff.

Simple adjustments can be easily made. Defer all major decision-making on any critical day, for you might make costly errors of judgement. Use the negative stages of your cycles for day-to-day routine matters. When in the positive phase, it should be easier for you to grasp new ideas and have the initiative to test them. Make those long, tiring business trips without drawing too much on your reserve strengths; you will certainly feel the better for it.

Plan meetings around your own biorhythms, especially meetings with those with whom you want to do more business. This is one of the new tactics used in some organisations by executives who have invested in a potential client's biorhythm calendar. They assess their degree of compatibility and, if these figures are not too favourable, find a colleague who *is* compatible and turn the case file over to him or her. In many cases, because you have an advantage over the opposition, it can only help you win.

When your physical rhythm is in a positive phase, you are able to maintain effort and energy without too much trouble. Keep up the momentum, push yourself and those who work with you to ensure you achieve your goals. If the physical rhythm is in its negative stage, take it easy, learn to delegate where possible, do not overdo business lunches and make sure you get adequate rest. If you overdo it now, your body may rebel and let you down later, just at the wrong moment.

During the positive emotional rhythm stage, you should have the drive to carry out tried and trusted methods; it is also the best time to test out new theories. You are at your peak, so capitalise on it.

The emotional cycle's negative phase is best used to carry out routine matters, read through notes, and plan – but not too seriously. It is an excellent time to attend lectures and seminars, when all you have to do, as a rule, is take notes.

The intellectual rhythm's positive phase is best used for long-term planning or for preparing reports to be read by those who matter – the bosses. In the negative phase of this cycle, stick to routine; plod away at what is necessary to keep the wheels turning. Remember, there is just a chance that your memory may fail you, so stay out of the limelight.

Follow these simple rules and your personal performance will be greatly improved; this can only lead to more responsibility and promotion.

Travelling on Business

One of the many trials and tribulations of successful business professionals lies with their travel arrangements. Many of the problems may be alleviated if you are being driven, or are using public transport. Whatever the stage of any of your rhythms, the trick is to ensure that your comfort and well-being are properly catered for, so always allow more than enough time for travel; then after a particularly trying journey, you can rest up before your business commitment.

Driving the company car, or any vehicle for that matter, is more for personal convenience than anything else. Cost and safety are very important factors but, with judicious planning, driving need never be a trial.

Consult your personal biorhythm calendar before you make travel plans, and you will soon learn to choose the most propitious times. Avoid long journeys when any of the three rhythms are in a critical phase, positive to negative or negative to positive. This is especially so when the emotional rhythm is in a critical stage. You are easily irritated, become short-tempered and take more chances than normal. Waiting in traffic jams, even at the lights, is a bore. You are liable to miss a gear, stall the engine or not see the jay-walker you would normally spot on any other day.

On an intellectually critical day, parking can be difficult and you may be unable to gauge gaps between other vehicles properly. On a physical critical day, poor overtaking techniques tend to be the main problem. More accidents involving speed occur to those whose physical rhythms are in critical phase than at any other time.

The best time for long car journeys is when your intellectual rhythm is in the negative stage, but the physical and emotional rhythms in positive stages. You will not feel tired, even after a long trip, and you will be much easier to get along with. As long as you are aware of your biorhythms and compensate accordingly, all your journeys can be peaceful and safe.

Diet and Slimming

The vast majority of us leap on to a set of scales at the wrong time of the day, week, month or year and wonder where all those extra pounds have come from. Crash diets are often the immediate 'answer' for many; no bread, potatoes or sticky buns, ease off the drink and take more exercise.

The results can be rather dramatic: one minute the body is being abused and over-indulged, the next it is hardly being cared for at all. If this approach is followed when you are in the wrong stage of your physical rhythm, it can cause serious health problems. With careful planning, however, you should be able to stay with a sensible, well-thought-out regime to help you lose weight. You should make up your biorhythm calendar for three or four months or so in advance, and highlight your emotional and intellectual critical days. Try to start the diet about seven or eight days before the first of the critical days is due and, if possible, in the middle of the physical plus phase. Try not to wait too long for the 'ideal' conditions or you may never start!

You have to be careful what you eat on physical critical days. Make sure you eat only special 'diet-type' meals: ignore the high-starch foods like bread, potatoes, doughnuts or cream buns. If you feel you cannot do without a nibble, prepare a few lettuce leaves, a raw carrot or a stick of celery or two. Only on this one day should it really be necessary.

As each of the critical days comes along, you might find the diet hard initially. Strengthen your resolve during the first few critical days – then it gets easier. Monitor what you eat and stick only with what you know will do you good. Resist any temptation to binge, because that is probably an emotional cry from inside and will occur more often at an emotional critical period than at any other.

As the diet progresses, so will your feeling of contentment and well-being. By working with your biorhythms in this way, you will create a successful diet regime – and one that will work.

On an intellectually critical day, in either direction, make sure you do not become forgetful and start nibbling absent-mindedly – a definite symptom of an intellectual critical time. On a physical critical day, the strongest desire is to fill your stomach with any food you can lay your hands on. You feel you have had enough and want to end the torture. Recognise the warning signs, stick with the diet, and it all gets easier in time.

Remember, each critical period you get through helps you maintain this new behavioural pattern of eating properly, so you will become slim and stay slim!

Stop Smoking for Good

Smoking of any kind, at any level, is an addiction and is closely associated with the way people eat. People tend to put on weight when they first stop smoking; they nibble more to help fight the body's craving for nicotine.

However, you must plan effectively and create a well-thought-out campaign to free the system of this craving. This will require a properly timed exercise to ease the problem – but you must really *want* to stop.

With the help of biorhythms you can, but it will still not be easy. Make up your chart for at least one month; two would be much better. Time your start for about two or three days after a positive to negative critical day in the sensitivity cycle. At this time you are unlikely to experience much change in the way you feel. This will allow nearly two weeks before the next critical day, when you are most likely to weaken to temptation.

Try to be a few days into the early stage of the positive phase of the intellectual rhythm as well, but that is not so important.

You are better fitted to resist temptation and you should also be physically able to cope. Now, stop smoking!

By the tenth day, or nearly two weeks, you will be expecting your next physical critical day. It ought not to have too much of an effect, especially as it does not last very long. If you can stop smoking for a day, you can do it for two, then three, and so on. After that, a week is nothing, and in a month, with the intelligent use of biorhythms, you will have stopped.

Do remember that in the first few days of this exercise you will experience a change in your digestive system. Your body will want more food and drink than usual. If you do eat or drink a little more to compensate, do not worry too much, any small weight rise is a part of giving up smoking.

Sport

To be successful at any sport, outdoors or indoors, you should be aware of your individual biorhythm stages at all times. Of course, much depends on the sport you are involved in. For example, golf, archery, shooting and snooker require good visual skills, whereas boxing, football, running and swimming all rely on good physical stamina.

All sporting activities need the three biorhythms to be in their positive stages but, obviously, this is not always practicable or possible. A positive physical rhythm with a high or low emotional or intellectual cycle will need careful monitoring.

Once again, you should have your personal biorhythm chart set up well in advance, because proper planning is essential if you are to succeed in your particular sport. If all three of your cycles are in the plus phase, you are likely to overplay your hand; too much exuberance and lots of energy can lead to an uncontrolled situation. That all your energies are in the right stage is fine, but to control them effectively is another task.

When all three biorhythms are in their negative stages, then only your best efforts are going to mean anything. You may not set the world on fire, but with careful planning, you can still give a good showing and still win. With one or two rhythms in their critical stages your performance will be either brilliant or erratic. Both seem to occur in far too many cases.

Tennis players can balance their biorhythms to good effect. A low physical cycle can be cleverly used with a positive stage intellectual cycle to cut out distractions. Tennis players have to rely on themselves and their own skills to survive. They can work wonders if they have their personal biorhythm calendars to refer to.

Effective Studying

Not all of us are physical fitness fanatics, nor are we too worried about our weight. Thus, for those who are more involved with intellectual concerns, here are a few guidelines on how to improve study and prepare for examinations using biorhythms.

To study properly and efficiently will bring its own rewards but it is not always easy to find the time or maintain a disciplined approach to learn new matters or revise the old.

Crash courses are not recommended: they do not work and can lead to poor health, especially if you stay up half the night. If you are in a low physical stage, or on a critical day in any of the three rhythms, you can easily upset your digestive system.

Study and revision periods are best undertaken when you are in a high physical phase, for you will have lots of stamina for such prolonged sessions. The active or plus intellectual phase is the best time for absorbing new ideas and new information.

However, when the intellectual cycle is in its negative stage most people seem to study the best. This is the prime revision period. The mind is not really interested in new matters; it is happy just to jog along in neutral. The mind is much less perceptive, but you can still learn new things, though not with the same ease as when the intellectual cycle is in the plus phase.

Most actors and actresses study and learn their lines and new roles when their intellectual cycle is in the negative stage. Police officers have found this a good period in which to go over old files and review how far their caseloads have progressed. Their detection rate peaks more in this period than at any other time.

Sportsmen, however, do not do too well. They normally rely on their physical stamina perhaps more than intellectual prowess, but even they need to keep their wits about them; even champions lose occasionally. And it could have been because they were in their negative intellectual phase – and were not aware of it.

Health and Illness

In recent years, some medical authorities have begun, perhaps a little reluctantly, to acknowledge that biorhythms have some value in health matters. It has been found that the times of certain incubation periods between exposure to, and actually suffering from, a few childhood ailments may correspond with the physical cycle's critical days.

Colds and flu seem to tighten their grip on positive to negative physical critical days, and it has long been known that people recover more quickly from surgery when in the positive stage of their physical rhythm. In surgery, bleeding is more profuse on physical critical days.

You should try to make an appointment with your dentist when all three cycles are in the positive phases. When the physical rhythm is in the negative stage you are likely to feel more pain – and not just while visiting the dentist. A fall, a minor injury, a simple headache, all seem more painful at this time. Should the emotional cycle also be in the passive stage, pain can feel far worse than it actually is, because of your low level of emotional resistance.

Heart attacks and strokes occur more when both the physical and sensitivity cycles are critical or in the low phase. It does not follow that this *will* happen, however, it is only more likely to happen when you are in poor health.

Accidents

Accidents occur more frequently on single or multiple critical days because people are likely to be overconfident. When their rhythms are in the positive phase, just before a critical day, they are prone to talking themselves into, and out of, all kinds of situations. Equally, people can so easily misread the signs when they are in their negative stages and do not always take into account all the facts before they commit themselves to a course of action, that an accident can easily happen. When it does, the incident may not cause a physical injury. It could just as easily be a wrong business decision that leads to severe troubles in other ways.

One of the main causes of accidents to adults in the home is falling, especially where elderly people are concerned. Older folk are more prone to falls in the early hours or after a short nap. As people grow older, their metabolism does not come into full play until they have been awake for some time. They should wait a little before attempting to rise, and not make too many sudden movements. They are more likely to experience a fall on a critical day in their physical cycle than at any other time, so they should allow time for their autonomic nervous system to become properly adjusted.

Much the same goes for children, for they also become prone to accidents in the home on critical days in their physical rhythm. Equally, it could be the result of the adult in the home leaving things lying around on an intellectual critical day. It is so easy to misjudge things or be forgetful at these times.

Do-it-yourself enthusiasts fall prey to accidents on critical days, as a rule when their emotional or physical critical days move from the positive stage to the negative. Accidents are also likely to occur on their positive mini-critical intellectual periods. Many people talk themselves into delusions of adequacy at such times – and pay the price later.

The biorhythmic cycles control performance in our main areas of behaviour, that is, physically, emotionally and intellectually. However, it must be stressed that while they have no direct cause and effect in themselves, they are, in each case, subject to the prevailing conditions of the environment at a specific point in time.

Thus, these biorhythmic cycles are a potential answer to our 'on' and 'off' days. The intelligent use and awareness of the phase of the rhythms can provide a more positive approach to life and, after a short time, you will not experience so many of those unfortunate little incidents and accidents – you will begin to feel far better in yourself.

Relationships

Most of us try to get along as best we can with those around us, but it can be difficult at times. In our early childhood, family relationships are very important: they help to shape our basic attitudes and help us form associations with others of the same age as we grow older.

When an active youngster has a tantrum on a critical day, it can so easily lead to an accident. At the very least it will affect the mood of the parents and, should one or both not be in a compatible mood, it will lead to domestic disharmony.

Children do not have the developed sense of awareness that most adults should have, so, once a parent becomes aware of the effect that biorhythms might have on their children, it is a relatively easy matter for them to plan ahead and allow for such potentially difficult days.

If biorhythms can be used to help plan a more structured approach to family relationships, then parents should have their child's biorhythm chart created. At the very least, it can only lead to a more reasoned response on critical days. Armed with this advance warning, parents can avoid confrontational, hostile or unproductive moments and be more accommodating at such times. They are not being asked to change their overall attitude, but simply to make small adjustments; to be more understanding, not only of themselves, but also of their children.

This works just as well in reverse. Children will begin to see their parents in a better light, and it will help them understand that some adults can be reasoned with in times of stress.

When we become adults, our relationships are really not that much different, except that we ought to be able to control our moods a little better than when we were children. All relationships are crucial to our lives in one way or another.

Ordinary friendships rely on some kind of compatibility. When we call in at the newsagent's shop for our morning paper and cigarettes, we may indulge in mild banter, the level of which depends on how well we know each other. At work, associations are more likely to be on the intellectual level – we have to maintain 'face'.

Sex Drive

When it comes to love, sex and marriage, we need to be responsive at the right moment and be prepared for our partner at the right time. Our personal sex drive is governed in a cyclic manner in much the same way as any rhythm, and most people think, wrongly, that this is linked with the physical rhythm. Certainly people are more inclined to feel sexy and are likely to need or have sex when their physical rhythm is in the plus or positive stage than at any other time.

However, if your sensitivity cycle is in the negative phase, your enjoyment may not be as high nor your responses as enthusiastic. If the intellectual rhythm is also negative, 'automatic' sexual activity may upset your partner. On double critical days, your personal response to physical desire can lead to accidents, so caution in more ways than one is strongly advised!

Couples who are trying for a child may like to know that statisticians have found that biorhythms may be linked to the sex of a child. Women seem more likely to have sons when conception occurs while she is experiencing the positive phase of her physical cycle and the negative stage of her emotional rhythm, than at any other time. More girls tend to be born if conception takes place during the mother's low physical cycle and a high emotional cycle. If conception takes place when both the physical and emotional cycles are in the positive or negative phase together, it is not possible to predict the outcome with any reasonable success.

As the time approaches to give birth, pregnant women may be able to assess the date and time this is likely to occur using their biorhythms. The older the mother-to-be, the more likely the baby will arrive on an intellectual critical day. Natural birth is more likely to occur when either or both of her physical and emotional critical days are due. Should all of the mother's biorhythms be in their positive stages, birth is often an 'easy' matter; in any case, it is much more helpful if her physical biorhythm is positive. On an emotional critical day, she is liable to be more worried or tense than usual. This is likely to affect the delivery and make things more difficult.

9

The Rhythms of Life

It is interesting to note that critical days, especially in the physical cycle, often coincide with poor health and even death. It has been statistically recorded that these switch-over days are much more likely to be accident-prone than the non-critical ones, so the watchword should be caution. Critical days, of course, do not actually cause death, but they often coincide with it.

Perhaps the best analogy is an electric light bulb; if it has a weak filament, the most likely time for it to blow is at the precise moment it is switched on. The act of switching it on causes a burst of power to surge through the filament. Conversely, the bulb is just as likely to blow as it is switched off; one moment it pulses with life, the next there is nothing. Rapidly switching a light bulb on and off often has this effect.

Anticipating Dangerous Periods

Biorhythms can be used to anticipate potentially dangerous periods in life, however healthy the subject may appear at the time. It does not necessarily follow, however, that if you have a heart attack or are suffering from a disease that is known to kill, the next critical day will be your last. Far from it.

In hospital it would be ideal if the biorhythms of patients could be displayed at the foot of their bed, alongside the other charts used to monitor their progress. Shortly before their critical biorhythmic stages, an additionally alert watch could be kept on them – just in case.

The physical biorhythm is important, but so also are the sensitivity and intellectual rhythms. When faced with difficult decisions, it is important to have a clear mind, unclouded by emotional issues, and be free to operate without fear or favour. Throughout history, many awkward, terrible or splendid moments in people's lives have depended on their being emotionally free, and having unbiased thought.

However, certain figures from the past, famous or infamous, made decisions and carried out actions at either the right or wrong moment, as they saw it at the time. When we look at their biorhythms, we can sometimes see what might have caused them to take the actions they did and, more to the point, why they acted as they did.

Bonnie and Clyde

Perhaps one of the most infamous criminal partnerships of all was that of Bonnie Parker and Clyde Barrow who became the subject of Hollywood film folklore, songs and other highly suspect tales. In fact, they were hard-faced killers who, in their short reign of terror, were responsible for taking 12 lives (possibly more), and injuring many others as they embarked on their final stealing career across part of the south-west United States.

How they met, became lovers and partners is told elsewhere but, if we look at their biorhythms, it is easy to see how they became so enamoured of each other.

Bonnie was born on Saturday 1 October 1910 and Clyde was born on Wednesday 24 March 1909. Their physical compatibility rating was quite high, 65 per cent. Their sensitivity and intellectual compatibility ratings were slightly higher at 71 per cent and 70 per cent respectively, giving them an overall assessment of 69 per cent.

Physically, each would have actively encouraged the other in turn, with first one and then the other initiating physical activities. Their sensitivity rating was good for most of the time but it is known they had vicious displays of temper occasionally. Intellectually, they worked together well, with each knowing the other's personal foibles and how the other would react in times of great stress or while just resting.

On Wednesday 23 May 1934, the Louisiana state police set up an ambush following a series of armed raids over a relatively short period of time in parts of the south-west of America. Parker and Barrow drove straight into it and died in a hail of bullets. The police later said that they were hit more than 50 times.

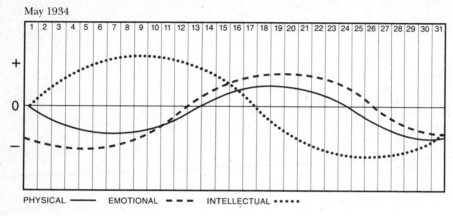

Figure 15. Bonnie Parker for 23 May 1934

Bonnie's biorhythms for this day were quite unfavourable – she was about to experience a physical positive to negative critical day. In addition, her intellectual rhythm was almost at rock bottom. She was, therefore, physically off balance, emotionally unstable and intellectually down. She simply was not thinking straight at all and did not recognise the danger signs.

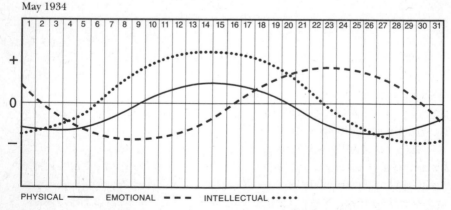

Figure 16. Clyde Barrow for 23 May 1934

Clyde's rhythms were even worse: tired and physically under par, he was unable to think clearly because, while his emotional rhythm was at the high point, his intellectual rhythm was on a critical day, positive to negative. He, too, failed to recognise the danger signs and paid the price for it – rightfully, of course.

Eva Braun

The long-time mistress, companion and, finally, wife of Adolf Hitler died in the bunker in Berlin alongside her husband of just a few hours some time during Monday 30 April 1945. She was born on Tuesday 6 February 1912, in Munich.

There has been much speculation as to whether she was murdered, either by Hitler or an aide loyal to the last, or if she really did commit suicide.

April 1945

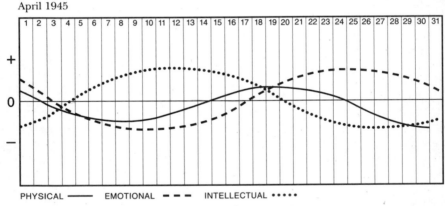

PHYSICAL ——— EMOTIONAL – – – INTELLECTUAL •••••

Figure 17. Eva Braun: died 30 April 1945

The victims of violence rarely show disturbed biorhythms unless their own actions were the cause of their trouble. Thus, if she was murdered, the chances are that her biorhythms would appear relatively normal, but if she took her own life, they would show some disturbance.

Her biorhythms for that day were poor. The day she married Hitler she experienced an intellectual mini-critical day – the cycle was at its absolute nadir. Furthermore, on May Day, she was approaching a similar position in her physical cycle, along with an emotional critical period.

In addition, Eva Braun was a woman who suffered from depression and, once or twice, these dark periods got the better of her. On the day of her death, her biorhythm chart showed how badly disturbed she was.

She had previously tried to commit suicide on 1 November 1932, and her chart for that day shows her biorhythms to be almost as unbalanced.

November 1932

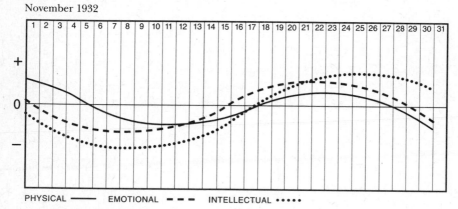

PHYSICAL ——— EMOTIONAL — — — INTELLECTUAL •••••

Figure 18. Eva Braun: first suicide attempt, 1 November 1932

Some three years or so later, on 29 May 1935, she again attempted suicide; again her biorhythms reflect her emotional and mental state.

May 1935

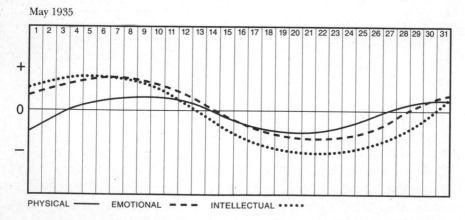

PHYSICAL ——— EMOTIONAL — — — INTELLECTUAL •••••

Figure 19. Eva Braun: second suicide attempt, 29 May 1935

The day before the attempt she experienced an emotional critical period; the day after, she was intellectually critical. So, with this evidence to hand, when we come to review 30 April 1945, we have to believe she really did take her own life. Her biorhythms did not cause her to do so, but they do reflect the prevailing conditions of her immediate environment at the time of her death.

This is just one example of how a figure may be drawn from history and their thoughts and actions judged anew, using their biorhythms.

President John F. Kennedy

It does not always rest with politicians to make decisions that alter a nation's destiny. When Lee Harvey Oswald shot President John Kennedy on Friday 22 November 1963, one cannot blame the President for an act that was virtually outside his control.

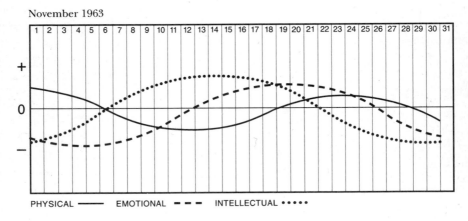

Figure 20. President John F. Kennedy: assassinated 22 November 1963

It was not a direct action by the President himself that caused his death. However, when we come to survey his biorhythms for that fateful day, an interesting conclusion is reached. It is now known from all the information collated in the later investigations that, although Kennedy had been advised of the possibility of an assassination attempt, he chose not to heed the warnings.

Born on 29 May 1917, his biorhythms for the day on which he was assassinated were up physically and emotionally, but at a critical stage in the intellectual cycle. Perhaps he was feeling a little overconfident about his popularity as a result. This could have been the reason he decided not to take advantage of a covered, bullet-proof vehicle.

President Abdel Nasser

Gamal Abdel Nasser of Egypt died suddenly of a heart attack on 28 September 1970. He was born on 15 January 1918. At the time of his death he was about to experience a double critical period in the physical and sensitivity cycles over the next two days.

If he was overdoing things, his timing was obviously wrong. The use of biorhythms would have advised him that he was just two days past an intellectual mini-critical period. He was liable to think he could cope with whatever he was given, and easily tempted to take on more than usual.

September 1970

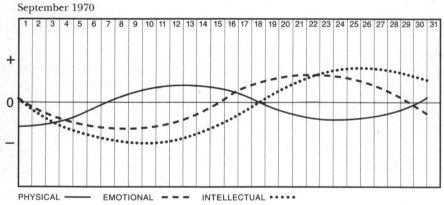

PHYSICAL ——— EMOTIONAL ▬ ▬ ▬ INTELLECTUAL •••••

Figure 21. President Nasser: died 28 September 1970

With a double critical period imminent, he was not tempting fate as such but he would have been well advised to ease off. If he had been aware of his biorhythms, he might have taken a different course of action on that fateful day.

Clark Gable

Clark Gable, often called the King of Hollywood, who was born on 1 February 1901, suffered his first heart attack on 5 November 1960. When we look at his biorhythms for this time we can see that he had just experienced a critical emotional period on the previous day and, on this day, was undergoing a physical critical period.

November 1960

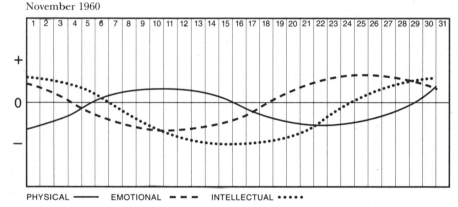

PHYSICAL ——— EMOTIONAL – – – INTELLECTUAL •••••

Figure 22. Clark Gable: died 16 November 1960

He had his second, fatal heart attack on 16 November, another physical critical day, but this time he was switching from the positive to the negative phase. He was also one day away from an emotional critical day, with his intellectual rhythm in negative phase. Obviously, his biorhythms did not cause him to die, but their condition was not helpful either.

Terry Waite

The Archbishop of Canterbury's special envoy in the Middle East disappeared rather mysteriously while on a mission in Beirut on 20 January 1987. Terry Waite, who was born on 31 May 1939, and was famed for his special negotiating abilities in this hotbed of intrigue, had just undergone a physical critical day.

He was on a positive to negative emotional critical period when he was kidnapped. Could his biorhythms have caused him to misread the signs or to be overconfident, leading to his own long period as a captive? Would he have made the same decisions that he did make if he had known what his biorhythms were?

January 1987

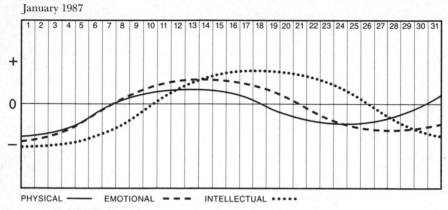

PHYSICAL ——— EMOTIONAL – – – INTELLECTUAL •••••

Figure 23. Terry Waite: kidnapped 20 January 1987

Alan Ladd

Alan Ladd, another film favourite, who was born on 3 September 1913, died suddenly on 29 January 1964. At this time he was in the middle of a double critical period in his physical and emotional cycles.

January 1964

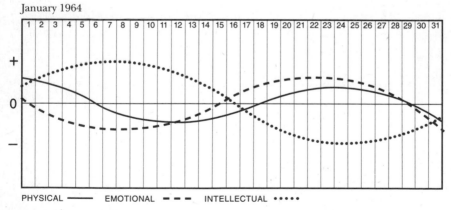

PHYSICAL ——— EMOTIONAL – – – INTELLECTUAL •••••

Figure 24. Alan Ladd: died 29 January 1964

Judy Garland

Judy Garland, who was born on 10 June 1922, died of a drugs overdose on 21 June 1969. Not known for her good health at the best of times towards the end of her life, she was just two days past an intellectual critical day, from positive to negative, and was on an emotional critical day, also positive to negative. She was due to experience a physical critical day on 24 June.

June 1969

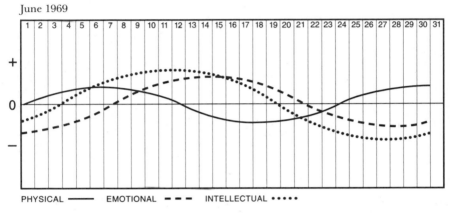

PHYSICAL ——— EMOTIONAL — — — INTELLECTUAL •••••

Figure 25. Judy Garland: died 21 June 1969

Harold Wilson

Born on 11 March 1916, he first became British Prime Minister in 1964 and had an interesting political history until his sudden resignation was announced on 16 March 1976.

March 1976

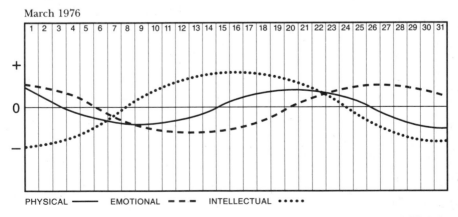

PHYSICAL ——— EMOTIONAL — — — INTELLECTUAL •••••

Figure 26. Harold Wilson: surprise resignation 16 March 1976

His biorhythms for that day show that he had just experienced a negative to positive physical critical day and that he was on a mini-critical intellectual day in the positive phase. This may throw some light on why he acted as he did. It might have been a bluff to his colleagues, or perhaps he just threw everything up on a whim. Perhaps the official papers will throw more light on the matter when they are made public in due course.

Indira Gandhi

The Indian stateswoman and the first woman Prime Minister of her country was the daughter of Jawaharlal Nehru, himself a former Prime Minister. Born on 19 November 1917, she became the victim of assassins, members of her own personal Sikh bodyguard, on 31 October 1984.

Her intellectual rhythm was in a critical stage, passing from the negative to positive stage. Mrs Gandhi did not always listen to advice from those who put her interests first. That may have been a contributory cause of her death.

October 1984

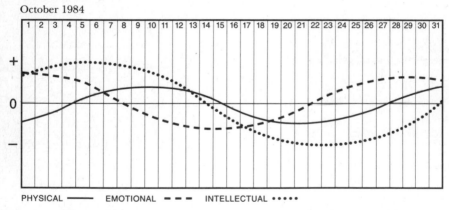

PHYSICAL ——— EMOTIONAL — — — INTELLECTUAL •••••

Figure 27. Indira Gandhi: assassinated 21 October 1984

Pope John Paul I

He was born Albino Luciani on 17 October 1917 and elected pope on 26 August 1978. Some 33 days later, late in the evening of 28 September, he allegedly suffered a heart attack and died as a result, but was not found until the very early hours of the following day.

Rumours soon abounded suggesting foul play, partly because of his highly original approach to the papacy, and also because there was no post mortem. His biorhythms were quite normal and do not suggest poor health.

September 1978

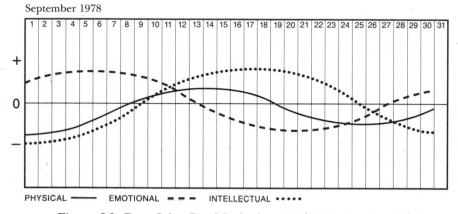

PHYSICAL ——— EMOTIONAL — — — INTELLECTUAL •••••

Figure 28. Pope John Paul I: died on 28/29 September 1978

Given all the circumstances, the accusation that he was poisoned may have some substance. He was an ordinary, practical man, full of common sense. Who knows what political enemies he may have made in so short a time, or what struggles he might have had if he had lived?

Mark Spitz

Mark Spitz, born on 10 February 1950, achieved immortality when he created a still-unbeaten record by winning seven gold medals at the 1972 Olympics, held at the end of August and the beginning of September.

His biorhythms were at double peak form and must have contributed considerably towards his outstanding success. Between 27 August and 8 September, Spitz notched up his extraordinary total almost within the space of a single week.

On 27 August, he had experienced a double critical in the physical and intellectual cycles and another double critical, this time in the physical and emotional cycles, a few days later, on 8 September: surely a possible explanation for his enormous success.

August 1972

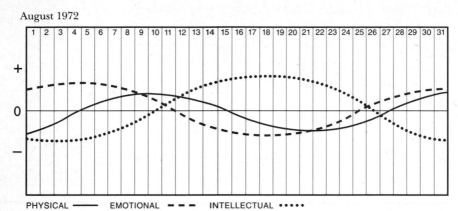

September 1972

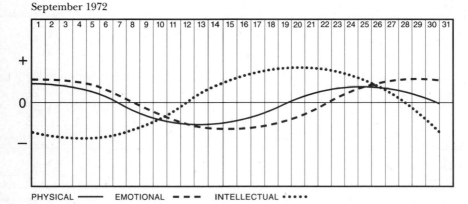

Figure 29. Mark Spitz: Olympic performance late August/early September 1972

Neil Armstrong

Without a doubt, the most momentous occasion of the century did not take place here on Earth, but it was certainly a very special 'Earth man' who stepped out on to the surface of the moon on 20 July 1969.

Neil Armstrong, who was born on 5 August 1930, set foot on the moon with the immortal words: 'That's one small step for a man, one giant leap for mankind'. He had blasted off on 16 July, on a physically critical day, perhaps an inappropriate day for an event entailing so much physical stress.

He then experienced a triple mini-critical day on 22 July and had to undergo the enormous physical stress of re-entry on 24 July. Despite the phasing of his physical cycle, his two other rhythms were in absolutely peak form for balanced judgement.

Remember, Neil Armstrong had to take over the controls and land the lunar module. There could be no dress rehearsal and, in those historic eight days, his rhythms were just about perfect for such a task.

July 1969

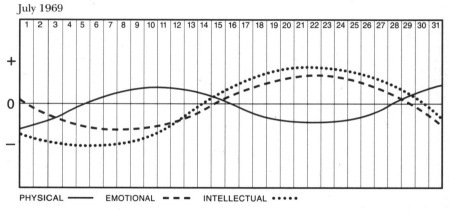

PHYSICAL ——— EMOTIONAL — — — INTELLECTUAL •••••

Figure 30. Neil Armstrong: landing on the moon, 20 July 1969

Because of the lack of gravity involved, he would not have needed too much physical strength, except for the beginning and end of the journey. However, a razor-sharp mind and emotional balance were essential for a successful mission.

Here was something that no other man had ever done before. Just what would happen when he actually landed on the moon had to be in the realms of pure speculation. In the event, it represents a case of perfect biorhythmic timing.

Kenneth Williams

Actor, comedian, raconteur and wit, Kenneth Williams was born in London on Monday 22 February 1926. He kept personal diaries for many years, providing us with a detailed record of the events of his daily life and also his reactions to them, which we can now compare with his biorhythmic charts.

At the end of his life he noted almost daily that he was in great pain from a number of causes. In several of his last entries he refers to his hope of an operation to alleviate his suffering. His biogram for the day he died shows that all his rhythms were in their negative stages and he was just two days away from a positive critical day. It was all too much for him.

April 1988

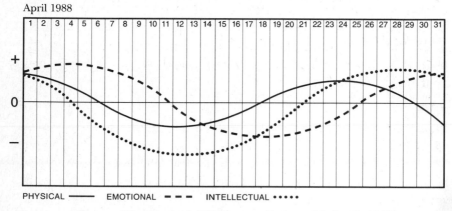

PHYSICAL —— EMOTIONAL – – – INTELLECTUAL •••••

Figure 31. Kenneth Williams: died on 15 April 1988

Is This Your Day?

Now let us look at the combinations of positive, negative and critical stages within our own biorhythms and how they may affect our lives. Each rhythm passes through the three phases of their respective cycles every few days or so, either in the positive, negative or critical stage. In the critical period, they may change from negative to positive, or positive to negative. So there are 27 different combinations that everybody experiences at any one time.

The following assessment of all these continuously interweaving variations and the recommendations of what to do and what to expect of them, should be regarded as guidelines only. Remember, we are all different, and we do not all react in quite the same way to any given set of circumstances.

Key: **A** = positive phase
   B = negative phase
   C = critical day

The cycles are referred to in the accepted order – physical, then emotional, then intellectual.

AAA:
This is quite clearly a good day all round and nothing should be beyond you. Objectives can and will be achieved easily, so go all out for what you want. Plan today in advance and be creative for, if you do not, while you may feel good, you may not have anything to show for it.

AAB:
Physically and emotionally you feel on top of the world – but a word of caution: your judgement is below par. Take care; what may look good on the surface might not fulfil its promise. For best results, let today be one for having fun and mixing with your friends. Work to first impressions, rely on your instincts.

AAC:
Your physical and emotional approach will be quite positive; you are in fine form. However, you could be a little overconfident and liable to make a few mistakes here and there because you are on an intellectual critical period. This means you are slightly accident-prone, so take care.

ABA:
You will be inclined to feel a little 'out of it', although physically you will be in fine fettle. Your mental capacity is quite receptive, so you are best suited to intellectual pursuits of all kinds. Keep your social contacts to a minimum as far as possible. The 'lone wolf' approach might be one answer.

ABB:
Physically, you probably feel quite fit and ready to tackle some of those odd jobs or get out into the garden, play games or go for a long hike. Leave the social niceties for another time and do not trust your judgement too readily. Do not commit yourself to any new or long-term project.

ABC:
An awkward period in which you are probably unable to think in a logical manner. Physically you feel fine, and can get along with most tasks that just need a gentle hand on the tiller. You are inclined to be a little restless, and co-ordination could be a problem. It would be best just to let things happen as they will.

ACA:
A feeling of overconfidence is probable. You can achieve your aims but, because you are liable to feel easily irritated with those around you, lose your temper, or fail to understand the way others work, it could be an accident-prone day. There may also be a lack of concentration.

ACB:
Physically, you are quite able to take on all manner of activities, but if you have to think about matters for too long you may easily make the wrong decision. On an emotional critical day you are prone to being at odds with people at the drop of hat. It is you who will be out of step. Take care, study or revise notes.

ACC:
Another high-risk period. You have an excess of energy but poor control and are apt to talk yourself and others in and out of all kinds of problems because you are so off balance, perhaps more than you think. Your confidence and ability are impaired and, on this critical day, you are accident-prone.

BAA:
The mind is willing but the body is not. Any heavy physical activity should be kept to a bare minimum, for your emotional and intellectual cycles may perhaps make you feel too confident. Just keep up with social and mental pursuits without getting too tired. Plan with care, the important things first.

BAB:
This could be a highly creative period. Work on your hobby or spend time with friends. Energy levels may be a little on the low side and you may be unable to sustain your concentration for long periods. Allow those around you to dictate the pace of things and just let things happen as they will.

BAC:

This is an accident-prone day and, while only your emotional outlook seems to function properly, you will probably feel out of sorts. On top of all this, it is also an intellectual critical day, so your judgement is likely to be clouded; some decisions may be questionable.

BBA:

Try not to let your mind take too much control of everything. You will not feel too sociable, so curl up in front of the television set or read; you may not suffer fools gladly. If you must be with others, hold back a little and keep physical activity to a minimum. Avoid confrontations; keep a low profile.

BBB:

You may as well take it easy and relax. There is little point in starting anything new, for even extra-special efforts may not last, however hard you may try. Use the time for revision or study. Actors should learn their lines; sportsmen should practise.

BBC:

Keep a low profile and concentrate on recharging your batteries. This is an accident-prone period. You are physically down and may not be too sociable either. Furthermore, you will probably be unable to think straight, so do not take risks and avoid taking short cuts, no matter how good they might look.

BCA:

A low physical cycle coupled with a critical emotional day means you may be accident-prone. A high intellectual cycle suggests certain abilities but, with the emotional cycle critical and the physical cycle down, there will be problems in achieving your aims. Take care when driving or handling unfamiliar tools and equipment.

BCB:

Don't do anything hasty and stop to think before you act. A wrong decision now may cost you dear later. You are physically and intellectually 'down' on an emotionally critical day. This is another accident-prone day; keep travel to a minimum and let others do the driving.

BCC:

This is a particularly poor day, with both your emotional and intellectual rhythms in critical phase. Take care in everything you do, because your physical rhythm in its low stage just makes things worse. Avoid physical activity and, should you have to travel, double-check your plans.

CAA:

Try to avoid the challenge of too much physical activity: moving house or digging over the garden are not recommended. On an emotional and intellectual positive day you may feel you can do it all, but this could prove to be your undoing as you do not have the energy. You are accident-prone – don't forget it.

CAB:

You will be far from your best. While your perception is high you will feel sluggish physically. Your co-ordination may suffer and lead to avoidable mishaps. In your eagerness to please others you could overlook details you might otherwise not miss. This is a time for adjusting to what others might want.

CAC:

You will experience an abundance of confidence together with an inability to read the signs you might normally observe. You will be off balance because both the physical and intellectual cycles are in their critical phases. Socially, you may go a trifle over the top. Your feelings may be rather intense.

CBA:

A depressing sort of day. You can become tired easily and, as you feel low emotionally, your overall outlook is not too bright either. You must keep your mind clear at all times, for you are prone to being distracted at the wrong moment and this can lead to an accident. You will be at your best on your own.

CBB:

This is another accident-prone short period, so do take care. You will be off balance physically and not as perceptive as normal and, on top of this, you may be tempted to take on much more than you can reasonably be expected to handle. You might not see the error of your ways until it is too late. Safety first!

CBC:

A very trying and irritating period when, whether you like it or not, it is you who are out of step with everyone else and not the other way around. Your negative emotional rhythm is not able to cope properly with the other two cycles in their critical phases. This really is an accident-prone day.

CCA:

You are liable to think without allowing for alternatives. When the emotional and physical cycles are in their critical phase and the intellectual cycle is positive, your judgement becomes clouded. Serious mistakes can occur just when you least expect them. Think things through carefully.

CCB:

You are liable to feel sluggish physically. Your perception and emotional reactions are slow. When your physical and emotional rhythms are both critical, you are prone to accidents. Your moods will range from low to high and you are unlikely to see problems looming until it is too late to do anything about them.

CCC:

Exceptional caution must be taken in all you do. Your rhythms do not coincide like this very often but, when they do, you really must make every effort to remain cool, calm and collected all the time. The slightest thing can set you off, so stay on the straight and narrow and avoid all temptations not to do so.

Remember, all the above conditions usually last only a day, but there are occasions when some of the combinations may affect you for 24 hours, or even more in some circumstances. As a rule, this tends to happen more with the plus or positive stages than with the negative periods.

Your Personal Chart

Now is the time to create your personal biorhythm chart so you can be ready to make the simple adjustments necessary to put you in better control of your destiny.

You have all the information you need in this book to set up your personal biogram, and all the interpretative material to help you make the right decisions.

If you wish, you may also go back to look at dates when you made certain decisions and acted in a certain way. You can do so, not only for yourself, but for those close to you, your idols, living or dead, or for historical figures. It is quite possible that biorhythms may have all the answers – or at least a part of them.

Either way, looking ahead, it never hurts to plan and prepare properly for those special times when extra attention to detail will make all the difference between success and failure.

10

Celebrity Birth Dates

Listed here are the birth dates of over 300 individuals from all walks of life – crime, entertainment, history, politics, sport – who have made a specific mark, for good or evil, in the pages of history by their deeds, thoughts or words.

Whether your motivation stems from professional interest, serious study or just plain curiosity, you will be fascinated to discover why famous people from past history up to the present day behaved in the way they did on a particular occasion.

Every effort has been made to ensure that the list is accurate. Inclusion here means that several different published sources have been consulted for verification.

Caroline Aherne	24 December 1963
Prince Albert	26 August 1819
Louisa M. Alcott	29 November 1832
Princess Alexandra	25 December 1936
Muhammad Ali	18 January 1942
Woody Allen	1 December 1935
Ursula Andress	19 March 1938
Prince Andrew	19 February 1960
Julie Andrews	1 October 1935
Princess Anne	15 August 1950
Antony Armstrong-Jones	7 March 1930
Paddy Ashdown	27 February 1941
Fred Astaire	10 May 1899
Rowan Atkinson	12 January 1955
Alan Ayckbourn	12 April 1949

Lauren Bacall	16 September 1924
Douglas Bader	21 February 1910
Brigitte Bardot	28 September 1934
Ronnie Barker	25 September 1929
Clyde Barrow	24 March 1909
David Beckham	2 May 1975
Sir Thomas Beecham	29 April 1879
Alexander Graham Bell	3 March 1847
Tony Bennett	3 August 1926
Ingrid Bergman	29 August 1917
Tony Blair	6 May 1953
Victor Borge	3 January 1909
Ian Botham	24 November 1955
David Bowie	8 January 1947
Charles Bronson	3 November 1922
Pierce Brosnan	16 May 1953
Richard Burton	10 November 1925
James Caan	26 March 1939
Marti Caine	26 January 1945
Michael Caine	14 March 1933
Al Capone	17 January 1899
Pablo Casals	29 December 1876
Barbara Castle	6 October 1911
Fidel Castro	13 August 1926
Charles Chaplin	16 April 1889
Prince Charles	14 November 1948
John Cleese	27 October 1939
Bill Clinton	19 August 1946
Joan Collins	23 May 1933
Sean Connery	25 August 1930
Billy Connolly	24 November 1942
Robin Cook	28 February 1946
Henry Cooper	3 May 1934
Ronnie Corbett	4 December 1930
Marie Curie	7 November 1867
Timothy Dalton	21 March 1946

Jim Davidson	13 December 1953
Bette Davis	5 April 1908
Sammy Davis Jnr	8 December 1925
Doris Day	3 April 1924
Catherine Deneuve	22 October 1943
Diana, Princess of Wales	1 July 1961
Leonardo DiCaprio	11 November 1974
Charles Dickens	7 February 1812
Walt Disney	5 December 1901
Amanda Donohoe	29 June 1962
Kirk Douglas	9 December 1916
Sir Arthur Conan Doyle	22 May 1859
Faye Dunaway	14 January 1941
Bob Dylan	24 May 1941
Clint Eastwood	31 May 1931
Mary Baker Eddy	16 July 1821
King Edward VII	9 November 1841
Prince Edward	10 March 1964
Samantha Eggar	3 May 1939
Albert Einstein	14 March 1879
Dwight D. Eisenhower	14 October 1890
Queen Elizabeth II	21 April 1926
Queen Elizabeth, the Queen Mother	4 August 1900
Ben Elton	3 May 1959
David Essex	23 July 1948
Chris Evans	1 April 1966
Kenny Everett	25 December 1944
Peter Falk	16 September 1927
Ralph Fiennes	22 December 1962
Michael Flatley	16 July 1958
Henry Fonda	16 May 1905
Jane Fonda	21 December 1937
Dame Margot Fonteyn	18 May 1919
Glen Ford	1 May 1916
General Franco	4 December 1892
Aretha Franklin	25 March 1942

Lady Antonia Fraser	27 August 1932
Dawn French	11 October 1957
Sir Clement Freud	24 April 1924
Sigmund Freud	6 May 1856
Sir David Frost	7 April 1939
Stephen Fry	24 August 1957
Yuri Gagarin	9 March 1934
Greta Garbo	18 September 1905
Judy Garland	10 June 1922
James Garner	7 April 1928
Lesley Garrett	10 April 1955
Paul Gascoigne	27 May 1967
Charles de Gaulle	22 November 1890
Bob Geldof	5 October 1954
King George V	3 June 1865
King George VI	14 December 1895
John Glenn	18 July 1921
Gary Glitter	8 May 1934
Hermann Goering	12 January 1893
Michael Grade	8 March 1943
Steffi Graf	14 June 1969
Billy Graham	7 November 1918
Cary Grant	18 January 1904
Hugh Grant	9 September 1960
Larry Grayson	31 August 1923
Robson Green	18 December 1964
Germaine Greer	29 January 1939
Sir Alec Guinness	2 April 1914
Gene Hackman	30 January 1931
William Hague	26 March 1961
Tony Hancock	3 May 1924
George Harrison	25 February 1943
Prince Harry	15 September 1984
Goldie Hawn	21 November 1945
Sir Edward Heath	9 July 1916
Audrey Hepburn	4 May 1929

Michael Heseltine	21 March 1933
Damon Hill	17 September 1960
Sir Edmund Hillary	20 July 1919
Alfred Hitchcock	13 August 1899
Adolf Hitler	20 April 1889
Dustin Hoffman	8 August 1937
Sir Anthony Hopkins	31 December 1937
Harry Houdini	6 April 1874
Jacques Ibert	15 August 1890
Henrik Ibsen	20 March 1828
Vincent d'Indy	27 March 1851
Jeremy Irons	19 September 1948
Eddie Izzard	7 February 1962
Glenda Jackson	9 May 1936
Mick Jagger	26 July 1943
David Janssen	27 March 1930
David Jason	2 February 1940
Sir Elton John	25 March 1947
Tom Jones	7 June 1940
Carl Jung	26 July 1875
Danny Kaye	18 January 1913
Buster Keaton	4 October 1895
Helen Keller	27 June 1880
Gene Kelly	23 August 1912
Grace Kelly	12 November 1929
Felicity Kendal	25 September 1946
Nigel Kennedy	28 December 1956
Deborah Kerr	30 September 1921
Martin Luther King	15 January 1929
Ben Kingsley	31 December 1943
Henry Kissinger	27 May 1923
Burt Lancaster	2 November 1913
Angela Lansbury	16 October 1925
Mario Lanza	31 January 1921

Christopher Lee	27 May 1922
John Lennon	9 October 1942
Jerry Lee Lewis	29 September 1935
Liberace	16 May 1919
Abraham Lincoln	12 February 1809
Charles Lindbergh	4 February 1902
Maureen Lipman	10 May 1946
Franz Liszt	22 October 1811
Sophia Loren	20 September 1934
Joanna Lumley	1 May 1946
Shirley Maclaine	24 April 1934
Sir Paul McCartney	18 June 1942
John Major	29 March 1943
Peter Mandelson	21 October 1953
Princess Margaret	21 August 1930
Spike Milligan	16 April 1918
Bob Monkhouse	1 June 1928
Patrick Moore	4 March 1923
Roger Moore	14 October 1927
Eric Morecambe	14 May 1926
Kate Moss	16 January 1974
Lord Mountbatten	25 June 1900
Audie Murphy	20 June 1924
Pete Murray	19 September 1925
Jimmy Nail	15 March 1954
Admiral Lord Nelson	29 September 1758
Anthony Newley	24 September 1931
Paul Newman	26 January 1925
Jack Nicklaus	21 January 1940
Vaslav Nijinsky	28 February 1890
Leonard Nimoy	26 March 1931
Richard Nixon	9 January 1913
Rudolph Nureyev	17 March 1938
Merle Oberon	19 February 1911
Des O'Connor	12 January 1932

Paul O'Grady (Lily Savage)	14 June 1955
Maureen O'Hara	17 August 1921
Gary Oldman	21 March 1958
Lord Olivier	22 May 1907
Jacqueline Onassis	28 July 1929
Ryan O'Neal	20 April 1949
George Orwell	25 June 1903
Richard O'Sullivan	7 May 1944
Peter O'Toole	2 August 1933
Al Pacino	25 April 1940
Arnold Palmer	10 September 1929
Bonnie Parker	1 October 1910
Camilla Parker Bowles	17 July 1947
Dolly Parton	19 January 1946
Prince Philip	10 June 1921
Edgar Allen Poe	19 January 1809
Sidney Poitier	20 February 1927
Roman Polanski	18 August 1933
Enoch Powell	16 June 1912
John Prescott	31 May 1938
Elvis Presley	8 January 1935
André Previn	6 April 1929
Vincent Price	27 May 1911
Mary Quant	11 February 1934
Sir Anthony Quayle	7 September 1913
Caroline Quentin	11 July 1959
Roger Quilter	1 November 1877
Anthony Quinn	21 April 1916
Ronald Reagan	6 February 1911
Robert Redford	18 August 1937
Vanessa Redgrave	30 January 1937
Sir Cliff Richard	14 October 1940
Dame Diana Rigg	20 July 1938
Anita Roddick	23 October 1942
Ginger Rogers	16 July 1911

Mickey Rooney	23 September 1920
Diana Ross	26 March 1944
Telly Savalas	21 January 1924
Jennifer Saunders	12 July 1958
Peter Sellers	8 September 1925
William Shatner	22 March 1931
Frank Sinatra	12 December 1915
Boris Spassky	30 January 1937
Barbara Stanwyck	16 July 1907
Ringo Starr	7 July 1940
Tommy Steele	17 December 1936
Patrick Stewart	13 July 1940
Barbra Streisand	24 April 1942
Peter Stringfellow	17 October 1940
Gloria Swanson	27 March 1899
Chris Tarrant	10 October 1946
Dame Kiri Te Kanawa	6 March 1946
Margaret Thatcher	13 October 1925
Terry-Thomas	14 July 1911
Jeremy Thorpe	29 April 1929
Marshal Tito	25 May 1892
Mel Tormé	13 September 1925
Paul Tortelier	21 March 1914
Lana Turner	8 February 1920
Twiggy	19 September 1949
Leslie Uggams	25 May 1943
Galina Ulanova	10 January 1910
Liv Ullman	16 December 1939
Tracy Ullman	30 December 1959
Stanley Unwin	7 June 1911
Captain Charles Upham	21 September 1908
Mary Ure	18 February 1933
Peter Ustinov	16 April 1921
Rudolph Valentino	6 May 1895

Eamon de Valéra	14 October 1882
Frankie Vaughan	3 February 1928
Ralph Vaughan Williams	12 October 1872
Robert Vaughn	22 November 1932
Jules Verne	8 February 1828
Queen Victoria	24 May 1819
Gore Vidal	3 October 1925
Lindsay Wagner	22 June 1949
Clint Walker	30 May 1927
Sir Barnes Wallis	26 September 1887
John Wayne	26 May 1907
Ruby Wax	19 April 1953
Raquel Welch	5 September 1942
Orson Welles	6 May 1915
Oscar Wilde	16 October 1854
Prince William	21 June 1982
Kenneth Williams	22 February 1926
Barbara Windsor	6 August 1937
Duchess of Windsor	19 June 1896
Duke of Windsor	23 June 1894
Ernie Wise	27 November 1925
Victoria Wood	19 May 1953
Anthony Worral-Thompson	1 May 1952
Michael York	27 March 1942
Susannah York	9 January 1942
Andrew Young	12 March 1922
Gig Young	4 November 1917
Jimmy Young	21 September 1921
Darryl F. Zanuck	5 September 1905
Franco Zeffirelli	12 February 1923
Catherine Zeta-Jones	25 September 1969
Ferdinand Zeppelin	8 July 1838
Mai Zetterling	24 May 1925
Efrem Zimbalist Jnr	30 November 1923
Emile Zola	2 April 1840
Pinchas Zuckerman	16 July 1948

Blank Charts

You can photocopy these charts for your own use.

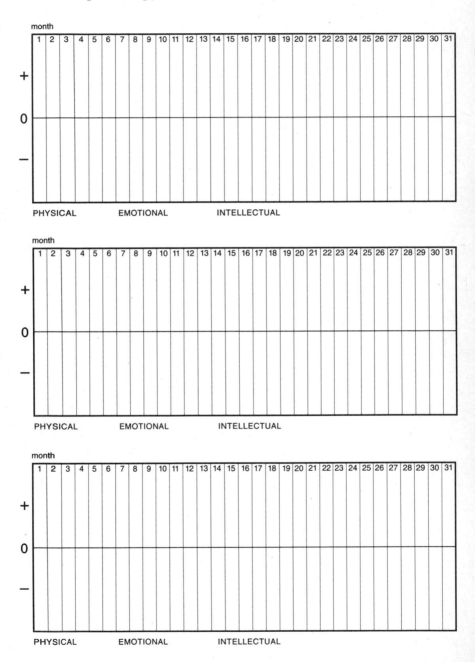

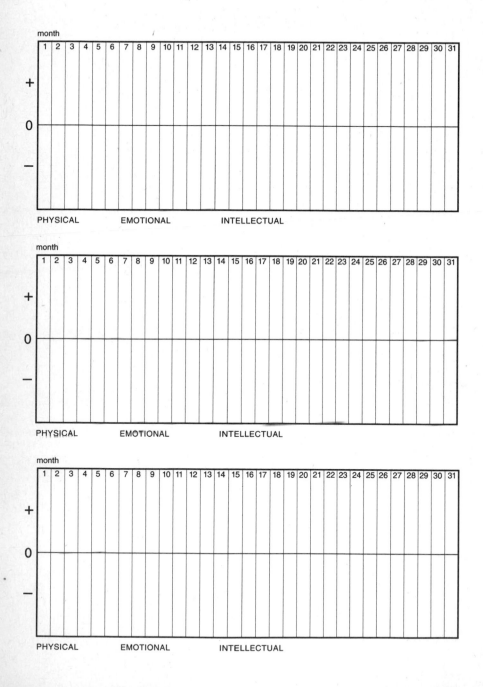

Suggested Further Reading

Jeremy Campbell, *Winston Churchill's Afternoon Nap*, Aurum Press, 1986

Edward R. Dewey, *Cycles*, Hawthorn Books, 1971

Bernard Gittelson, *Biorhythms*, Arco Publishing Company Inc., 1976

Hugo Max Gross, *Biorhythms*, Modern Press, 1976

Gay Gaer Luce, *Body Time*, Granada Publishing Limited, 1973

Don Rebsch, *Biorhythms and You*, Universal Biorhythm Company, 1977

Rosemary Stewart, *Best Days of Your Life*, Pyramid Publishing, 1977

Kichinosuke Tatai, *Biorhythms for Health Design*, Japan Publishing Inc., 1977

George Thommen, *Is This Your Day?*, Crown Publishing, 1973

Hans Wernli, *Biorhythms*, Crown Publishing, 1961

Index